Sister M. A.

Poems for Catholics and Convents and Plays for Catholic Schools

Sister M. A.

Poems for Catholics and Convents and Plays for Catholic Schools

ISBN/EAN: 9783742833648

Manufactured in Europe, USA, Canada, Australia, Japa

Cover: Foto ©Thomas Meinert / pixelio.de

Manufactured and distributed by brebook publishing software
(www.brebook.com)

Sister M. A.

Poems for Catholics and Convents and Plays for Catholic Schools

POEMS

FOR

CATHOLICS & CONVENTS,

AND

PLAYS FOR CATHOLIC SCHOOLS.

BY

THE SISTERS OF MERCY,

ST. CATHARINE'S CONVENT, NEW YORK CITY.

PERMISSU SUPERIORUM.

(Proceeds for the Benefit of the Children under the care of the Sisters.)

STEREOTYPED AND PRINTED AT THE
NEW YORK CATHOLIC PROTECTORY, WEST CHESTER, N. Y.
1874.

TO THE

SERVICE OF THE POOR,

AS IT MAY BE PROMOTED BY THE

PROTECTION, EDUCATION, AND TENDER CARE

OF THEIR

DEFENCELESS CHILDREN AND YOUNG DAUGHTERS,

THESE VERSES ARE AFFECTIONATELY

INSCRIBED BY

THEIR DEVOTED SERVANTS IN

OUR LORD'S LOVE,

THE SISTERS OF MERCY.

TO THE READER.

In offering this volume of unpretending verses for circulation in the Institutions conducted by Religious, and among Catholics in general, we are actuated by a two-fold motive: the desire of obtaining means to support the poor, dear children under our care; and the hope of eliciting a new interest and a greater zeal in behalf of suffering childhood.

No city in the world has done so much within the last ten years for the protection of its children, as New York; and the noble work done by the Catholic Protectory, and some other recent Institutions, may be pointed to as proof; yet the *Catholic World*, for November, 1872, tells us that there are still 40,000 homeless children in this metropolis exposed to every misery, "who tread the paths that lead to moral destruction with such rapidity, that hundreds of them are confirmed thieves or drunkards before they reach the age of twelve years." *

Yet every one of these forty thousand children is capable of being trained to Christian modes of life, to usefulness, to piety, and truth. Help us to help them.

---

* *Catholic World*, Nov. 1872, page 207.

Whoever buys a copy of this little book contributes to the great work, and may look for a reward to Him who has said: "Whatsoever you do to the least of these, my little ones, you do it unto Me."

What a joy to rescue a young innocent child from the haunts of vice and misery, and bring it up in ways of virtue and industry! Then, why are not the children rescued?

Alas! for want of means; for want of money.

Every little mouth must be fed, every tiny pair of feet must have shoes, and each one must be decently clothed, and these things cost money; ever so much money, when you have some hundreds of little mouths to feed, and twice as many pairs of restless little feet to keep covered. We defy fashion, *as far as we can*, but we admit that the philosophy of clothing is something wonderful.

You cannot teach a child to be self-respecting, well-mannered, and ready to work for a living, unless you clothe her properly; nay, you cannot induce her to be earnest in the practice of her religious duties; whereas, if you take the most wretched and neglected little creature and clean and clothe her, you have done, perhaps, as much to improve her in moral sentiment as in appearance.

Our aim, as Sisters of Mercy, is to catch the children before they fall into habits of vice, before they have been corrupted by the influence of evil example: and the children in our Institution are all of this class.

We design to educate them respectably, to teach them useful trades, to train them up in habits of virtue and piety; and so to fit them to become blessings to society and models of good example among their friends.

Every aid given to enable us to accomplish this task will be highly appreciated, and no doubt amply rewarded, for it is one of the best of all good works; one of those charities dearest to the Heart of that all-merciful Saviour who said: "Suffer little children to come unto Me, and forbid them not." Ah! but the world forbids them; the world and the flesh and the devil forbid them in a thousand ways, and it is for you, Catholic people, —fathers and mothers of happy home-loved children, to help them to come; it is for you, young men, young girls, with all life's enjoyments, to brighten each hour of your existence; it is for you to reach out your hands to the little sufferers, and help them over the thorny paths their poor young feet are treading.

Yes, it is for you, children of the rich, —little boys and girls who never knew a want, —it is for you, numerous, happy band that you are, to help those who have no mother's heart to rest upon, —no father's kindly smile to sweeten the bitterness of their lonely child-lives. Our Lord loves a cheerful giver; if you spare some of your pocket-money to help our little ones to have a better dinner, to be more comfortably clothed, or to have a better bed to sleep in; if even from the number of cast-off garments and toys grown distasteful to your feasted eyes, you spare a mite to those to whom these things would be like rays of sunlight, —you may be sure, you will enjoy your own comforts with lighter and happier hearts, while your bright Angel will be ever presenting your gifts before the throne of One whose love will for ever overshadow, and bless, and surround you, both here and hereafter.

A word about the verses themselves. Some of them were printed a few years ago in different Catholic Journals; some of them, viz., those peculiarly referring to country and kindred, were composed before their writer entered the Convent, and none of them were expressly written for publication.

The book is divided into two parts, of which the second is suited only for children, and school purposes. In days when literature is used so powerfully against the interests of the Church, may not even these poor verses be tolerated as being, at least, wholly and devotedly Catholic ?

SR. M. A.

CONTENTS.

PART FIRST.

POEMS FOR CATHOLICS AND CONVENTS.

PART SECOND.

POEMS AND PLAYS INTENDED FOR CHILDREN ONLY.

PART FIRST.

POEMS

FOR

CATHOLICS AND CONVENTS.

POEMS

FOR

CATHOLICS AND CONVENTS.

LINES

COMPOSED BEFORE WRITING A PETITION FOR MEANS TO
AID IN ERECTING A HOME FOR HOMELESS CHILDREN.

SACRED HEART of Jesus! fill my mind with light,
Give me words of wisdom, guide my pen aright;
For Thy homeless children, Jesus, I appeal,
Make me wisely utter what I warmly feel.

Once before, Lord Jesus, I essayed to aid
Homeless little children, to Thine image made;
Then I failed, unworthy and unfit and weak:
More unfit, less worthy now, yet must I speak.

Speak to men, Lord Jesus, men of wealth and pride,
Seek to turn their interest from the world aside,
Reach their hearts and win them to expend their gold
On the lambs that shiver in the wind and cold.

Use me for this service, send me love divine,
Jesus, Jesus, Jesus, make these children Thine;
Shelter them, Sweet Jesus, to Thy robe they hold,
Shelter them and save them, to Thy heart enfold.

Suffer little children close to Thee to come,
Help us to provide them shelter, comfort, home;
They are Thine, Lord Jesus, bless the words I say,
Draw them to Thy service, guide them on their way.

ROSA LEE.*

Rosa Lee was but a baby
    When her mother died of grief;
Hopeless sorrow crushed her spirit,
    Death she sought for as relief.
Rose, her fair, young, helpless daughter,
    Love-deserted and unblest,
Never hid her infant sorrows
    In a mother's loving breast.

Soon they left her, heartless strangers,
    In the streets where outcasts roam,
But the empire city's mercy
    Gave the little one a home.
A home where home affections
    Never find a resting place,
A home where homeless children
    Live, the aliens of their race.

Little Rose! Her eyes were bluer
    Than the azure depths of sky,
When the birds seek their siesta,
    For the sun is summer high.

---

* These verses were written before the children of Randall's Island were
allowed to receive Catholic instruction, and when there was no institution for
poor Catholic children except the Orphan Asylums.

And her baby curls were sunny,
　　Though her fair young face was wan;
Little Rose, all pale with sorrow,
　　E'er those baby years were gone.

Rosa Lee, she grew a beauty,
　　Unbaptized, unblest
With the grace that tells of heaven
　　As the haven of our rest.
No loved finger pointed upward,
　　No kind voice had ever warned
Poor young Rose, without religion,
　　All her young affections scorned !

Rosa Lee, her heart was loving
　　And it grew more loving still,
But, alas ! for no one loved her,
　　All around were dark and chill.
Not so Rose.　Her life grew dreamy,
　　And within her refuge home
How the bright world shone before her,
　　How she longed through it to roam.

Once or twice a mouldy novel
　　Found its way into her hands,
And she dreamed of wealth and freedom
　　And of love-enchanted lands;
Of the flowers, and of the forests,
　　Of the bird-songs and the bees,
Of the silvery rivers, shadowed
　　By the old time-honored trees.

Rose read on, a world of wonder
　　Rushed at once upon her mind;
Love and life and hope together
　　In these pages seemed entwined.

Poor young Rose, her home a prison,
  And her heart imprisoned too,
And without a guide—forgive her,
  For she knows not what to do.

She grew wild—unbridled fancy
  Bore her on its wings away,
And she fled her childhood's shelter
  In the flowery month of May.
See her enter the great city
  Dreamy, beautiful, untaught;
Life, a mystery she knows not,
  With temptation overwrought.

Rosa Lee—alas, I dare not
  Trace her footsteps farther on,
For she treads the path of ruin,
  And she treads it not alone.
Soon, too soon, she's like her mother,
  Only that she does not *die*,
That she finds a harder fortune
  While despair is looming nigh.

O Lord Jesus, Blest Redeemer!
  There are hundreds like to Rose,
Round them circles of temptation
  Like a reeling vortex close.
They are stainless still, Lord Jesus!
  Childhood's light is in their eyes,
Give us *love enough* to save them,
  Hear their heart-appealing cries.

In their *names*, the voice of Erin,
  In their veins, her martyr-blood,
Yet they're borne to dark perdition
  As on some wild, sweeping flood;

Carried on to vice and horror,
  Borne away from faith and hope,
Flung like waifs upon a torrent,
  With its seething waves to cope.

Move all Christian hearts, my Savior,
  With a mercy like to thine;
Let them rest not, till they raise thee
  For thy little ones a shrine;
A home for homeless children
  Full of pity, full of love,
Love of Jesus, love of Mary,
  Hope of bliss with them above.

A home for homeless children,
  Sacred to thy Sacred Heart,
.Where their young lives shall be cherished
  With affection's mother-art.
And then a home in heaven,
  Where around Thy glorious throne
Our rescued little children
  May form a radiant zone.

ON THE PRESENTATION OF THE BLESSED VIRGIN.*

BLESSED Virgin! Mary! Mother! thou art now a little child,
Earthly stain hath not approached thee, Adam's sin hath not defiled;

---

* Composed in the Cathedral of Albany during the ceremony of its Dedication, which took place on the Feast of the Presentation, 1853, and suggested by Father Noethen's wonderful singing of the *Magnificat*, particularly the verse, "Deposuit potentes de sede."

To the temple thou art coming, there thy pure young life
    to give
Unto Him in whom all creatures have their being, move,
    and live.

Never one like thee hath trodden o'er Judea's flowery
    sod,
For the angels to attend thee hasten from the throne of
    God;
All heaven's choicest gifts they bring thee, Faith and
    Hope and Love divine,
All its graces, all its virtues make thy purest heart their
    shrine.

Meekly that young head is bended, softly that low prayer
    is heard,
Which to hasten man's redemption rises daily to the
    Lord.
Yes, that prayer hath pierced the heavens; lo! the clouds
    drop down their dew,
To the thirsty earth He cometh, He who maketh all things
    new.

Little dreamest thou, sweet Mother, of the glorious day
    to be,
When the Lord from heaven descending, shall take flesh
    and blood of thee;
Little of thy bitter anguish standing by His Cross to see
All that sacred blood expended, shed for sinners, shed
    for me.

Little of the glory Jesus had reserved for thee above,
Where thou reignest now in mercy, Mary, Queen of
    holiest love!

Now that heart is heaven's treasure, now those radiant
    hands diffuse
Gifts and graces which we sinners oft so hopelessly
    abuse.

Now the nations bend before thee, and thy one loud song
    of praise
Is reëchoed wheresoever Christian hands their altars
    raise;
For the Lord hath raised the lowly and the proud to earth
    hath cast,
He hath come, hath "dwelt amongst us:" all the ancient
    types are past.

Blessed Mother, be a mother to us exiles struggling here,
In these days when hope and promise tremble into doubt
    and fear:
For the scattered sons of Erin pour thine all-command-
    ing prayers,
Make them heralds of salvation, and of heaven the right-
    ful heirs.

ADORATION ON THE FIRST FRIDAY.*

I RAISE my eyes, my Savior, and I see thee leaning there
On thy Mother's breast, a baby, with bright eyes and
    golden hair,
Rounded arms and rosy fingers such as earthly children's
    are,
Ere the sorrows of existence all their sinless beauties mar.

* The Altar alluded to was that of the old chapel of St. Catherine's Convent
of Mercy, Houston St., New York, where there was a beautiful picture of the
Virgin and Child above it, and an *Ecce Homo* near.

Smiling there, so calm and gentle, on that pure and virgin
    breast,
Preordained before creation to be thy first place of
    rest.
Fain I'd raise my eyes to see thee, but they sadly seek the
    ground,
For those heavenly looks are piercing to my heart's lone
    depths profound.
They remind me how you blessed me with baptismal grace
    and light,
And that I, almost an infant, cast away that robe of
    white;
They remind me with what mercy Thou preservedst me
    through all,
Girt me round with grace and blessing, sent me many a
    loving call.
And I bow my head o'erladen with the memory of sin,
And a sorrow half delirious thrills my aching heart
    within.
Once again I look, Redeemer! God of might! oh, can
    this be
Thou whom Patriarchs and Prophets pined in ancient
    days to see;
Thorn-crowned and sorrow-laden, scourged, dishonored
    and defiled
As a would-be king derided—as a would-be God reviled?
Thou hadst led them out of Egypt, Thou hadst fed them
    from on high,
Yet they make the rough wood ready on which Thou art
    to die.
Not the Gentiles' blinded malice, 'tis thy chosen people
    who
Send these cries of "Crucifige," all the hills of Sion
    through.

Ah! I hear the *Ecce Homo* spoken through my inmost
    soul,
And the sorrows of the Passion like a tempest o'er me
    roll.
Let me gaze awestruck and humbled, for this work is all
    mine own,
I—a suppliant and a sinner at the footsteps of thy throne.
But again my eyes are lifted—ah! no pictured form I see,
Lovely in its faint resemblance of what Thou hast deigned
    to be;
But 'tis Thou, our blest Redeemer, all thy majesty and
    might
Shrouded in almost a nothing, finding with us thy
    delight.
It is He, the Babe of Bethlehem, it is Calvary's victim
    thus
With Heaven's divinest blessings concealed for love of us.
Oh! to see thee on that altar, earthly flowers to deck thy
    throne,
Earthly light to give thee lustre, who the true light art
    alone!
And to think that our poor homage should be incense to
    thy Heart,
And that *I* among thy children in its offering should have
    part,
Should have forced my heart to listen to that voice so
    clear and strong,
That recalled me from the desert ways wherein I wandered
    long!
This it is that overwhelms me, as I kneel before thy
    throne,
And perceive the little harvest of the seed so early sown.
Oh, for gratitude to bless thee! oh, for eloquence to praise!
Oh, for energy to serve thee in thy creatures all my days!

For the spirit of self-sacrifice, the glorious gift of love
To raise my heart this crowded world and all its cares
    above!
Give these to me, my Saviour, take all things else away,
And let me pass from death to life, from darksome night
    to day!
O Mary, Queen of mercy! let my heart be wholly thine,
Let love of thee and Jesus with all my thoughts en-
    twine;
Oh, clothe me with thy habit and screen me with thy
    veil,
And pray for me and aid me lest I fall away and fail!

ST. PATRICK'S DAY WITHOUT SHAMROCKS.

WE sought them 'neath the snow-flakes
    And o'er all the frosty ground,
But no leaflet like the Shamrock
    On St. Patrick's day we found.
And our hearts went back to Erin,
    To her dewy vales and hills,
Where the Shamrock twines and clusters
    O'er the fields and by the rills.

Oh, no more, no more, my Country!
    Shall thy loving daughter lay
Down her head upon thy bosom
    While she weeps her tears away.
There the primrose and the daisy
    Bloom as in the days of old,
And the violet comes in purple
    And the buttercup in gold.

But thy child, thine exiled daughter,
   She is far from thee to-day,
Dreary walls of brick surround her,
   Dreary miles of foreign clay.
For no home is hers, no country,
   Willville now is with the past,
On the chapel, on the graveyard
   She hath sadly looked her last.

Kildare's broad fields are fragrant
   With the Shamrock's breath to-day,
Shamrocks bloom from Clare to Antrim,
   From Killarney to Lough Neagh;
And they speak of Patrick's preaching
   With a quiet, voiceless lore,
And they breathe of Faith and Heaven
   All the trefoiled island o'er.

Wandering listless by the Liffey,
   Stoop and pluck the shamrock green;
What an emblem plain and simple
   Of the one true faith is seen!
Of the Father and the Spirit
   Speaks the mystic triune leaf,
Of the Son in anguish dying
   On the cross, in love and grief.

Well humility may choose it
   For an emblem fair and sweet,
Close beside the poorest cabin
   It is pouring fragrance sweet.
Modest is our darling Shamrock,
   Useful, charitable, kind,
Clothing mean, deserted places
   With its green leaves intertwined.

With the dew drops shining pearly
  As bright gems within its heart,
Pure as purity it seemeth,
  True as nature, fair as art.
Fortitude and perseverance
  Hath the leaf we love so well,
For 'tis green through all the winter
  In some shady nook or dell.

Many a lesson thus it teaches,
  Many a wholesome thought recalls,
Many a tear-drop all unbidden
  To its cherished memory falls.
For the green of Erin's banner
  Still must stir the Irish heart,
Which in Erin's many sorrows
  Ever, ever must have part.

Oh be true, be true to Erin,
  True to Faith and true to God,
To St. Patrick, his Apostle,
  Who redeemed your native sod!
Never more her mystic emblem
  In green Erin may you see,
Let the faith it symbolizes
  Be the dearer unto thee.

AN APPEAL.*

TO THE IRISH MILITARY COMPANIES OF NEW YORK IN
BEHALF OF THE DESTITUTE IRISH CHILDREN WHO ARE
NOT ORPHANS, AND FOR WHOM AS YET THERE IS NO
CATHOLIC ASYLUM.

———

The Green Flag proudly floating
　　Free in the foreign air,
By Irish hands uplifted,
　　And borne exultant there!
The Green Flag that our fathers
　　Have wrapped them in to die,
E'er sell their *faith* or *freedom*
　　Beneath their native sky.
　　　　　How gallantly, how fearlessly,
　　　　　　Their sons look here to day;
　　　　　The exile's heart is raptured
　　　　　　To see their proud array.

Homeward their thoughts are sweeping,
　　The old Green Land appears,
Wild sea-sought Connemara,†
　　And Wicklow's "Golden Spears." ‡
But passion fiercely rises
　　For over all the land,
Alas! they see in spirit
　　The prison poor-house stand.

---

* Written before either the Protectory or St. Joseph's Industrial School
was built.
† Connemara signifies, according to some, "The home of the sea."
‡ Mountains so called from their form and from the quantity of yellow-
blossomed furze with which they are covered.

Then gallantly and fearlessly
  They lift the Green Flag high,
And feel as if for Erin
  They gloriously could die.

Though now with hearts elated,
  They breathe fair freedom's air,
And fealty true and earnest
  To their new land they swear:
"America and Freedom
  Our ' homes and altars free,'
Our children, sons and daughters,
  We dedicate to thee."
      Yet mournfully, how mournfully
        Their voices falter now,
      For many Irish children
        'Neath sorrow's burden bow.

For many fair young children
  Of Irish birth or blood,
Are borne away to ruin
  On misery's fatal flood;
Are taught to hate their country,
  To curse their fathers' creed,
To think their names dishonor,
  Their Shamrock some vile weed.
      So mournfully, how mournfully
        The Irish music wails,
      The hearts it thrills are saddened,
        Their joyous spirit fails.

Oh save them! For the orphan
  A resting place is found,
A home where peace and comfort,
  And kindness all abound.

But for the widow's children,
  For those abandoned by
Their bad or reckless parents,
  Their refuge is to *die*.
     O lonely and neglected ones!
      'Tis you, 'tis you we seek,
     Let Irishmen but listen,
      But hear their own hearts speak.

To found a home for children
  Like these, is all we ask;
To care and keep and guide them,
  Be this our blessed task.
Build but a shelter for them,
  And loving hearts will aid
To save those helpless children,
  To ruin thus betrayed.
     O Irishmen! brave Irishmen!
      But aid us on our way,
     And rescued Irish children
      For you will often pray.

God in his own sweet mercy
  Will fill some hearts with zeal,
Will teach them for misfortune
  And want and woe to feel;
To be on earth His envoys,
  His messengers of peace,
To heal the hearts now breaking,
  The captive to release.
     Oh captive little children,
      Shut out from faith and love!
     His Sacred Heart will save you,
      And all your ills remove.*

---

* Written before the children on Randalls' Island were allowed to receive Catholic instruction, as they are so liberally at present.

He calls on you as Irishmen,
  As Christians, now to save
These little ones of Erin
  Whose home seems but the grave.
To rescue them—they're parted
  From home and peace and love,
They're lonely little exiles
  Where desolate they rove.
     Be merciful, be merciful,
       Men of the strong right hand!
     And save these precious relics
       Of our lost fatherland.

Oh ye who stood so boldly
  Alone, when all the crowd
Arose to honor England
  In pæans long and loud! *
Who neither fawned nor flattered
  But stood up for the right,
Come forward now and shelter
  These souls from evil's blight!
     'Twas English persecution
       That drove them to their fate,
     They're fragments of the "Famine,"
       They're wrecks of "Forty-Eight."

By the sunny hills of Erin,
  By the story of her wrongs,
By the rushing of her rivers,
  By the music of her songs;

* The Irish regiments who acted in a manner so creditable to themselves and to their country on the occasion of the "Prince's" visit.

By the shamrock's mystic meaning,
  By the love of home and hearth,
By the graves where sleep our fathers,
  In the sacred Irish earth;

By their faith that never faltered,
  By the blood her martyrs shed,
By the hope that lives within her,
  By the living, by the dead;
Oh, by all that stirs emotion
  In a nature noble, true,
Men of Erin, save her children!
  'Tis a glorious work to do.

Many in the cause will offer
  Time and labor, love and life,
Only give the means to save them
  From a world of sin and strife.
Nurture them as Christian children,
  Make them love their holy faith,
Fill them with the love of Jesus,
  For 'tis He Himself who saith:

"Whosoever then receiveth
  One such child, receiveth me;"
I will bless him in his labors,
  I his great reward will be.
And again He says: "But suffer
  Little ones to me to come,
For of such is heaven's kingdom:"
  Heaven is their truest home.

ONE GLIMPSE OF THE RUSHING WATERS.

ONE glimpse of the rushing waters,
  One thought of the flashing sea,
And away my thoughts go sweeping,
  Eastward all fast and free.
Not to the gorgeous Indies,
  Not to the Isles of Palm,
Not unto where the spice-trees
  Burden the air with balm.

But with the rushing waters
  On to an island lone,
Lone on the verge of Europe,
  Queenly but overthrown.
Queenly with grand old memories,
  Proud, for a thousand years
Are gone, since her name's first glory
  On history's roll appears.

Sorrowful as a mother,
  Seeing her children die,
Choking with shame, as chieftain,
  Seeing his spearmen fly;
Laden with all emotions,
  Filled with a passion strong
Stirring her, as a master
  Sweepeth the chords along.

On with the rushing waters,
  On to where Antrim's coast
Seeth their stormy power
  Scattered to foam and lost.

Round by the green soft headlands,
  Round by the mountains blue,
With the streams like veins of silver
  Gleaming and glancing through.

Round by Old Invercolpa,
  Where Boyne's ill-fated flood
Pours down its tide of memories,
  Tinged with the hue of blood.
Round by the hills of Wicklow
  Richened by song and tale,
Legends of ancient Glendalough,
  Songs of Avoca's vale.

Stilling my heart's wild motion,
  Staying the rising tears,
I gaze upon Howth's blue headland,
  Gaze on the "golden spears;"
Gaze upon old Killiney,
  Purple with bloomy heath,
Smiling down on the waters
  Murmuring far beneath.

Think of a day long perished,
  When over that hill I roved
Through all the summery splendor,
  Circled by those I loved.
Think of their true devotion,
  Think how it ruled my life,
Think to what steadfast purpose
  It moulded my being's strife;
Think of the deep, far future,
  Shrink from its weary years,
Vague without life's first purpose,
  Dim with subsiding tears.

Back with the rushing waters,
  Back with the ebbing seas,
Back to the strange Savannahs,
  And to the alien trees;
Leaving behind the well-spring
  Of hope, and love, and thought,
The home where with life's dull tissues
  Threads of fine gold were wrought.

ON SEEING AN ORCHARD IN BLOSSOM.

Now the orchard flowers are coming
  Once so welcome to our sight,
Apple-flowers so faintly blushing,
  Cherry blossoms pale and white;
Cherry blossoms, so luxuriant,
  Covering like a fall of snow,
Shining in the trembling sunbeams
  Every brown and polished bough.

Cherry blossoms, so luxuriant
  That the leaves are forced to wait
Till their wealth of bloom is scattered,
  In the sun to try their fate.
Apple-flowers, so soft and fragrant,
  So bepraised by bird and bee,
Wrapping old gnarled boughs so fondly,
  Decking gayly each old tree.

Ah! I knew a tree wide-spreading
  Flow'ry boughs o'er silvery grass,
An old gray tree, but now the summer
  Airs thro' all its being pass.

Down I sit 'mid blue bells bending,
  Weighty with the diamond dew,
Cowslips, polyanthus, primrose,
  Sweet in fragrance as in hue.

Down I sit, the clouds are passing
  Swiftly o'er the wading moon,
Soft white clouds by moon-rays gilded,
  Losing all their gold full soon.
Darksome valleys frown between them,
  There the constant stars still shine,
Stars that lift our thoughts to regions
  All unearthly, all divine.

But the white clouds, fringed and gilded,
  O'er their silver radiance roll;
Thus how oft do fancy's vapors
  Hide the true light from the soul!
Lone I sat me down to number
  O'er the luckless years I've known,
Since my canopy was flowers,
  Since the green grass was my throne;

Since the birds made all my music,
  And the bees my study were,
And my greyhound was my courtier,
  "Nimrod," he was surely there.
But the clouds again are coming,
  Clouds of sorrow, clouds that pass,
Like slow hearse-plumes, o'er the vision
  Of the flowers among the grass.

Oh beyond them, to the regions
  Bright with hope, still let me soar,
Hope not earthly, hope in heaven,
  There the will of God adore!

In the sky's dark depths the faces
  Of the stars are clearest seen:
In the depths of sorrow, Heaven,
  God, and Faith look most serene.

"HE CAME UNTO HIS OWN AND HIS OWN RECEIVED HIM NOT."

HE came unto his own, His chosen people,
  He came to those whom Moses led of old,
He came to breathe new life in Rachel's children,
  To gather the stray sheep of Israel's fold;
To heal the wounds of Abraham's descendants,
  To build up David's holy house once more,
To be the glory of the second temple,
  Jerusalem's true greatness to restore.

He came most humbly. Mary, Virgin Mother,
  Thy royal blood was veiled in humbleness,
And Joseph, the true son of David, labored
  Only to make his dignity seem less.
He came most humbly, all His glories veiling,
  And all His majesty, and all His might;
He came unto His own and they denied Him
  In this first hour a resting-place at night.

He came unto His own and they reviled Him,
  He came unto His own and they despised;
He heaped good things upon them and they slew Him,
  And the true words of life as folly prized.
Long weary years He labored for them, teaching
  The way to heaven, bringing light and truth,
The wonders of Eternity revealing:
  But they rejected Him, both age and youth.

For them He prayed, long, lonely nights of sorrow,
    Sorrow, for, ah! He knew their malice well;
For them His wondrous miracles, His teachings,
    His love, His mercy that no words can tell.
For them the writing in the sand that told them
    What only God had power to reveal;
For them the pardon spoken to the sinner,
    For them the ardor of His glorious zeal.

Oh, it was all for them! Beside the fountain
    For the Samaritan He waited long, —
But not so long, most merciful Redeemer!
    As Thou hast waited my return from wrong.
For them, His tears, as sadly He regarded
    That old Jerusalem, so long beloved ;
For them, the agony in that lone garden,
    His prayer at whose appealing Heaven was moved.

For them the last dread sacrifice, for dying
    He thought of Israel and He thought of me.
Ah yes! He thought of us — He died to save us,
    He died to break our chains and set us free.
He died for the wild Nomad, who to Ismael
    Traces his claim on Abraham's mighty line,
For Brahma's worshippers and Jove's adorers,
    For all who bow at passion's idol shrine.

In Him the Greek might find the type of beauty,
    Its author and its architect, its whole;
Beneath His sway the Roman seek true freedom,
    True independence of the human soul.
Yes, He is all to all, yet they deny Him,
    To choose a sordid and a world-wise lot;
He came unto His own and they denied Him,
    Unto His own and they received Him not.

And, oh! He comes to us, He comes all humbly,
  He lives among us hidden, oft forgot.
Alas! beloved St. John, He comes unto us,
  Unto his own, and we receive him not.
Ah! let me give my life to make atonement
  For the wild thoughtlessness of bygone years;
The door stands open, Savior! let me enter,
  Let be thine in penitence and tears.

AN APPEAL.

Have pity, my Creator! oh, have pity
  On the frail dust which thou hast filled with life;
Task not so sore the spirit thou hast kindled,
  It aches and quivers in this mortal strife.

Long, long ago, e'er youth's soft sunshine faded,
  A shadow fell that dimmed its pleasant light;
How hath it darkened and extended, weaving
  O'er all existence the dull lines of night.

Toilsome hath been my pathway from that hour,
  Many its sorrows, multiplied its cares;
In the fair field of life's bright early promise,
  How hath the wheat been lost amid the tares!

And now the changing seasons come with warning,
  Warning of change to come or which hath been,—
Warnings which shine amid the snows of winter,
  And are not hidden 'mong the branches green.

For I have known an April day when nature
  Smiled in its sweet, uncertain, shadowy bloom,
While sunk young human hearts in early anguish,
  Chilled and o'ershadowed by too dark a doom;

A May, when hope was poured abroad like rain-drops
  O'er all the surface of our island home,
Her resurrection seemed a certain glory,
  Her day of retribution almost come.

The apple trees were fragrant with soft flowers,
  The young corn shone all silvery in the sun;
The flax bent, heavy with its frail blue blossoms,
  And the "Lone Bush" its fairy wreaths had won.

Our old home, sacred to so many memories,
  Looked happy as if all our love it felt;
Yet 'neath that roof its stateliest son lay dying,
  And there a widow and her orphans knelt.

Again, a few swift years, and autumn wearing
  Her regal hues of purple and of gold,
Saw these from home and from each other exiled,
  That mother gathered into heaven's fold.

Ah! sad is earth, and sad is life, its radiance
  Fades into gloom beside that funeral urn;
Oh! from its aching hopes and vain aspirings,
  "Refuge of Sinners!" unto thee I turn.

To thee, to thee, I turn me, God of mercy!
  Let not thy strengthening hand from me depart;
Thou who hast worn our loving human nature,
  Sustain and guide this shrinking human heart!

LINES.

WRITTEN ON READING ENUL'S "PARTING FRIENDS."

WERE we not happier if we made no friends,
　　If like the sun we poured alike o'er all
The riches of the heart, and made existence
　　Bright with enjoyment,—scenes that but recall
Visions of hero story, strains of music,
　　Martial or wailing in a funeral key,
Pictures of unseen glories, hymns to freedom,—
　　Might not a life of such as these things be ?

Were we not happier if we could forget,
　　If the strong chain that memory wove might break,
If the heart-worship that had birth of old
　　Might cease within the heart its tale to speak ?
Oh the long broken circle that together
　　Drank the sweet wine of hopefulness and youth,
Were it not happier to forget than never
　　Meet once again ? O earth, how sad is truth !

Were we not happier if the past were never
　　Its busy phantoms more to give us back ?
The green, bright earth hath fresh untrodden flowers—
　　Why will we follow the old dusty track ?
Are not the dark Sierras full of grandeur,
　　And the soft vales with living waters green,
May not a new world and new glories blind us
　　To the dim light that shines from what *hath been ?*

I would that we might travel on in fancy
　　Into all realms that brighten in the sun,
Behold the glories of primeval forests,
　　And see the rivers where their life begun.

Alas ! 'tis all in vain, I stop to listen,
　　My heart beats quick, a well-known voice I hear,
My eyes are dim with tears, for they are resting
　　Upon a face unutterably dear.

Ah! they are coming all, the old home circle,
　　The loved, the trusted, they are here with me—
My God! I bless thee for this gracious hour
　　That gives me once again those eyes to see.
The blue, deep, thoughtful eyes so full of beauty,
　　The royal brow and the brown sun-lit hair;
Earth knows her now no more, but surely heaven
　　Is all the brighter since she too is there.

There, in the freshness of her life's young springtime,
　　And in the grandeur of her stainless soul,
And in the richness of her heart's affections,
　　And in the genius that hath found its goal,—
There, not alone, for God hath kept together,
　　In the gold bonds of friendship and of love,
The two whose graves the wild seas part asunder,
　　Whose cradled rest one angel watched above.

Graves! graves! for such as they were,—oh how vainly
　　We garner up affection, since a day,
A little day, may shatter, bring to ashes
　　That which to us was as the sun to May.
Our paths have lain apart, and now 'tis only
　　Thus that my heart may fully speak to thine;
For you the young leaves and the purple zenith,
　　For me the autumn and the day's decline.

For you, young life's effulgence and the fragrance
　　Breathing around you, and the gift to thrill
With your least touch our innermost affections:
　　For me the "Psalm of Life" is awful still.

Were we not happier if we sought the real,
  The grand, the beautiful, in heaven to find—
There where our loved ones are, were we not happier
  If all our thoughts with theirs were intertwined.

"LAST WORDS."
SUGGESTED BY A DEATH-BED SCENE.

I am going now, my own love, I am leaving thee alone,
Where many a care and sorrow on thy gentle heart is
    thrown;
I leave thee, but thou wilt gather the closer unto thy
    heart
The little ones, of my memory and of my being part.
Dear is the daylight dearer the old familiar earth,
Whence the many-colored flowers and feathery leaves
    have birth.
Strew them around me, dearest, roses of palest hue,
Emblems of all things lovely, quickly to perish too.
Think of me when the springtime comes with its
    countless leaves,
Think of me when the summer garlands of beauty
    weaves;
And through the long, lone winter think of the love
    gone by,
Pray that its true enjoyment yet may be ours on high.
Brothers, and ye my sisters, partners in life's young glee,
Think of me oft and offer to heaven your prayers for me.
Why to that sheltered graveyard, near to our child-
    hood's home,
And its monumental chapel, does mournful fancy roam?
Sister, farewell! in heaven your cherub boy I'll meet,
So lately laid by angels in love at his Saviour's feet.

Shall I tell him that thou art waiting in patient, hope-
ful love,
Till the Angel that calls thee "Mother" shall brighten
thy home above?
Mother! the boy so joyous once by our native Rhine
Soon shall be lying lowly, far from his land and thine.
Oh, the majestic river—the glorious fatherland!
Dimly their memories haunt me, holy and pure and
grand.
But to thee, to thee, my Father! Redeemer! Lord! I
come,
Oh make thy servant worthy to find in heaven a home!
Ah human love and sorrow! strongly ye move me still—
Father! to thee I leave them—blest be thy holy will!
Comfort my white-haired father, soften my mother's woe,
Bless all that ever loved me, pardon my harshest foe;
Strengthen and fill with comfort the heart I love so
well,
Guide her and be her refuge—I go, I go,—farewell!

THE INCARNATION.

"AND THE WORD WAS MADE FLESH AND DWELT AMONGST
US."

GREAT God! Eternal Spirit, Omnipotent, All-Just!
Oh is it Thou, Thy real Self, shrouded in human dust?
Is man of so much price as this, his love so very dear,
That Thou for him this lowly guise of mortal flesh shouldst
wear?
O holy faith! O holy faith! my trembling reason flings
Itself upon thee for support, to thee it soars and clings.
God! God eternal! God supreme! all gracious, loving,
mild,
The very God, Creator, Lord, is Mary's weeping child;

Is hers, is ours, is come to make "His Sacred Heart" our
    own,
Is come to lift us from the dust and place us near His
    throne.
The cold assails Him, Mary hears His low, soft, infant
    sighs,—
He, who hath weighed the winds* and cast the white
    snow where it lies.
The beasts, the meanest beasts are lodged beside Him in
    the cave,
O humbled, humbled Majesty! all this our souls to
    save!
All this, dear Lord! how little this to all Thy life of
    pain,
Thy years of toil, Thy hidden love, Thy life-blood shed
    like rain
For us! dear Lord, for us! for me! for me, alas! who
    gave
To earth and earthly things the heart, Thy mercy stooped
    to crave.
I did not think, dear Lord, dear Lord, I did not think of
    Thee,
Thy birth, Thy blood, Thy prayers, Thy tears—all, all
    were lost on me.
Thy realms, the realms of cloudless day, to me were dark
    as night,
The flowers I sought were of the earth, their fruit looked
    fair and bright.
Looked bright? but, oh! my God, I know their bitterness
    ere now
Deadly to me. as unto all, the fruit of Eve's fair bough.

---

* Job, xxviii, 25.

Alas! the recreant, coward heart that feared the narrow
    path,
Saw but its thorns, and never dreamed what "easy
    ways" it hath.
I have been grateful, I have loved with but too much of
    love
Those who have helped me, when my woes seemed all my
    strength above.
Grateful to them, but not to Thee, to Thee from whom
    came all,
Ah! at Thy feet abashed and pale, now let Thy creature
    fall.
For I am Thine! Thy Precious Blood can wash all stains
    away,
The power of Thy Almighty Word can lighten all this
    clay,
Can vivify, re-animate with superhuman strength
The fainting spirit, and proclaim it all Thine own at
    length.
"Turn thou, most blessed Advocate, thine eyes of mercy
    turn"
Upon the child of one who with thy Son's true love did
    burn.
For her sake, oh! forget me not, O Mary! pray for me,
Reject me not, reject me not, though late I come to thee.

EGOISM.

MERCIFUL God, is this the being nurtured
    'Mid all things beautiful and good and fair?
Is this the head thy gentle hand, my mother,
    Bowed to the holy Name in childish prayer?

Are these the rosy fingers, eyes whose gladness
  Seemed to defy the threatening hand of care;
Is this the child that, nestling in thy bosom,
  Played with the tresses of thy raven hair ?

Is this "the little Mistress"—she so circled
  By the fond love of Owen's faithful heart,
Which prized the heiress of her race's sorrows,
  And in them all would fain have taken part ?
Oh, is this she, who had such love for all things
  As even from all things won a fond return,
Who joyed in every joy, and in all sorrow
  With quick and active sympathy could mourn ?

Is this the child that, through the woodlands roving,
  Sought out for thee the first and sweetest bloom,
That knew each bud and bell and fairy blossom,
  And lived amid their odorous perfume ?
Who loved the birds and knew their names and natures,
  The places green and shadowed where they build,
In fragrant hedge, or flowery bough, or tree-top
  With the wind-voices musically filled ?

Is this the girl that loved the breezy hill-side,
  And 'mid the free air felt her soul expand,
That loved the quiet of the fragrant evening
  And gloried in the sunrise strong and grand ?
That musing wandered by the murmuring river
  And heard the dirge of Erin in its voice,
A mourning sound that quelled the gushing gladness,
  Prone, like the spring-birds, wildly to rejoice ?

That peopled the hoar ruins with such beings
  As fancy fables at its own sweet will,
And wreathed wild legends round them, as the ivy
  Wreathes and adorns them with its kindly skill ?

That to the broken column by the Liffey*
    Turned with uplifted eye and curious care,
Musing, "What thought was theirs who made it utter
    That *Sursum Corda* in a scene so fair ?"

Was it lest Liffey's music and the bird-songs
    Might seem too heavenly sweet for mortal ears;
Or lest a scene so beautiful, so holy,
    Might seem to us transcendent as the spheres ?
Again, again that laughing child before me
    Stands wild and loving, with her father's eyes;
Again, again to home and thee, my mother,
    Memory on magic pinion swiftly flies—

Flies to find all a void. The *Sursum Corda*
    Now hath a solemn meaning, and its tone
Lifts the bowed spirit upward as it bids it
    Seek only in God's heaven to find its own.
For thou art there—O mother, mother! bear me
    Still in thy heart, for me be still thy prayer,
I am thine own with all my sins and sorrows,
    Help me my life's *new* cross in peace to bear.

Help me, for now a thousand loving memories
    Rush to this heart thou knowest so wild and warm,
So strong, yet weak, like oak whose branches breaking
    Are borne to desolation on the storm.
But yet the tree lives on, till dews of heaven
    Come to reclothe it in its primal green,
And the sweet summer birds, hid in its verdure,
    Sing thanks for finding there so fit a screen.

---

* There is a broken pillar on the banks of the Liffey, in the grounds formerly belonging to St. Walstan's Abbey, near Celbridge, Co. Kildare, with the above inscription.

So may my spirit rise above its sorrows,
  So praise the Lord of mercy evermore!
For this, sweet mother! to our Mother Mary
  Pray, as you taught me in the days of yore.

SIMMINSTOWN.

I AM thinking of our old home where we dwelt long ago,
And in fancy its sweet scenes arise as vividly as though
I could see the flowers springing in the grass so soft and
    green,
And that patriarchal apple-tree above them as a screen.

I am thinking of the old house where we dwelt with
    hearts at ease,
With its antiquated gables, peering from the chesnut
    trees;
Of the window that was hidden 'mong the cherry blossoms
    white—
How their coming in the spring-time filled our spirit
    with delight!

And again I see the rose-bed, so covered o'er with bloom,
That the later buds to open their petals scarce had
    room;
And the laurels and laburnums and the fragrant lilac
    trees
With their load of early blossoms, wooed by the summer
    breeze.

And the great old-fashioned orchard, with its trees so
    large and wide,
Beneath whose clustering branches in play we used to
    hide:

Beside it lived old Philip, that we used to tease so then,
Making songs about his bower and his pretty daughter
    Jane.

Then our dog, our poor old Nimrod, so graceful and so
    fleet,
Whose wild, well-meant caresses often flung me from
    my seat;
And the filly that we rode on, and we tried her mettle
    too,
For you know we kept a squire, to urge her o'er the
    dew.

I am thinking of "the dark walk," with its solemn
    shaded air,
And the scattered gleams of sunshine upon the blue-
    bells there,
Where with our own peculiar spade, that we rescued
    from a thief,
We trimmed our beds of flowers, in those days so bright
    and brief.

Oh! that spade recalls old memories, still dearer and more
    true,
My first, my best, my own friend! 'twas given me by
    you;
And that thought awakes a sadder,—one that can never
    fade,
For it dwells within a bosom whose earthly hope it
    made.

But I cease, for now the tear-drops to my eyelids burn-
    ing start,
As the saddening thought o'ershadows all, that now we
    are apart.

Years, many, long, and bitter, have passed since last we
    met,
Yet those days, those scenes, those early friends I *never*
    can forget.

SÆPE EXPUGNAVERUNT ME A JUVENTUTE MEA.
(Ps. cxxviii.)

I HAD a friend in the bright, sunny spring-time
    That was my own in my far fatherland,
Who pored with me o'er Aladdin and Sinbad,
    And loved the works of fair Titania's wand.
That wandered with me by the shady hedgerows
    To find the sorrel-blossoms, frail and white,
To whom the coming of the early violet
    And crimson orchis was a true delight.

'Mong the green rings, where fairy feet had trodden,
    She sought with me the snowy mushroom's place,
Or in the dew of May's first fragrant morning
    Laved with unthinking glee her laughing face;
Where Liffey's soft and sparkling waters wander
    Through shallow channels o'er their colored bed,
Her rosy feet with mine have often ventured, seeking
    For pebbles, white and purple, brown and red.

With me, beneath the golden-boughed laburnum,
    She sang in gladness, or in grief she wept,
Or 'neath the blossoming of hawthorn bowers
    Her mimic school with mimic staidness kept.
For her the winter had bright holly berries,
    Fair laurustinus, and the Christmas-rose,
And frostwork, beautiful and strange as fancy,
    And there was wild delight in drifting snows.

A time there was, I mind it well, it deepens
Nor fades in memory's close embrace,
When all things pointed unto God, and bade me
In heaven seek beauty in its dwelling place.
Alas! my chosen friend, my guide and counsel,
Blinded my eyes and led me far astray,
And then she showed me newer, prouder beauties,
To new affections led the pleasant way.

Into the dazzling realms of ancient story
She led me, tearful for Cassandra's fate,
Proud with the proud, or beaten with the vanquished,
Or with the Roman triumph all elate.
Romance she gave me, with its wild heart-pictures,
Pity for fair Rowena, pride and grief
For the proud maid of Juda—for Corinne,
An interest, to which tears were but relief.

Gulnare's wild story, Kalid's self-devotion,
And Hinda's sea-swept tomb disturbed my rest,
And she, who by the blue takes flowery margin
Died plague-struck for her love, seemed very blest.
And yet I knew, I *knew* how vain and fleeting
Are earth's wild fantasies and wilder hopes,
An unseen hand still beckoned me to leave them,
A voice still called me from life's sunny slopes.

There was an ancient convent, poor and hidden,
Where but the poor were cared for and caressed;
Oh, what an impulse have I felt to seek there
The narrow way that leads to endless rest!
Day after day I passed it, young and joyous,
Filled with the love and hope and life of earth,
Yet never *once* without that strange, quick impulse
To rush within, that quelled the thought of mirth.

Alas! alas! that false friend, how she wielded
  My own heart's armory against me still,
With strong affection's chains to earth she bound me,
  And forged new links with unrelenting skill.
The love of home, the love of thee, my country,
  The strong devotion to my name and race,
The heart so little guarded, proud and reinless,
  Led me a long and wild and fruitless chase.

Led me from Him, who from empyrean heaven
  Stooped to our lowly nature and became
The outcast of the land, reviled, rejected,
  Laden with all the burden of our shame.
I knew it well, full well, and all that teaching
  The gentlest and the holiest could bestow,
Remorse upon my young heart preyed unceasing,
  Yet there I stood rooted to earth below.

Ah! this false friend was *I* myself, I only—
  My own strong, passionate, unbridled will,
That led me through long years a willing captive,
  And seeks to hold me in its thraldom still.
O God of mercy! break them, rend asunder
  These bonds of death, and let me fly to thee,
Oh, make me free with that most blessed freedom
  Wherewith the Son of God hath made us free!

HUGH O'NEIL.

OLD, very old, the memories,
  That crowd our native isle,
Where her ruined temples crumble,
  Where her flowery valleys smile;

By her famous old Blackwater
    Lives the name of Hugh O'Neil,
Hugh the gentle, Hugh the courtly,
    Hugh the leader of the Gael.

Benburb may ne'er forget him,
    Nor Portmore, for all around
His strong "Red Hand," his iron will
    With foemen strewed the ground.
O English Queen! your men were strong
    And terrible in mail,
But their veteran valor yielded
    To the squadrons of O'Neil.

Down to Munster, where the Spaniards
    Came their chivalry to lend,
With O'Donnell, brave as lightning,
    And as hot, behold him wend.
And the Southern land is pleasant,
    Desmond's harassed fields are fair,
And the Ulster heroes sorrow
    O'er the ruin brooding there.

Ancient castles, where O'Briens
    Ruled with hospitable sway,
Where McCauras waved their banners,
    Oft they passed them on their way;
Norman keeps and Danish strongholds,
    Learned retreats, and holy fanes,
And the Shannon's saintly islands,
    And the Geraldine's domains.

Here are Norman abbeys, founded
    For the Norman race alone;
Here are Irish abbeys, plundered,
    And defiled, and overthrown.

How the blackened homesteads round them
  Stirred their hearts to vengeance then,
And they vowed from foes to free them,
  Vowed these strong, true-hearted men.

Old, very old, the sorrows that
  Crowd our ruined isle,
For the stranger won the battle,
  *Won once more by fraud and guile.
Oh, behold him, Hugh the gentle,
  Hugh the fearless, Hugh the brave,
Setting out with all his household,
  But to seek a foreign grave!

O'er the stormy Northern Ocean,
  Through the blue Italian sea,
Home of Christian hearts, eternal,
  Glorious Rome, he reaches thee.
Reaches thee, an old man laden,
  Oh, with what a weight of woe!
What to him the Coliseum,
  What to him the Tiber's flow?

Not Egeria, when she wandered
  From Olympian heavens of old,
Could bring comfort to the monarch,
  He whose land is bought and sold!
And he wanders, blind with anguish,
  Where had wandered hero bands,
Men like him of haughty spirit,
  Men who conquered many lands.

Men who breathed an inspiration
  Into history's pictured page,
Raised up monuments to freedom,
  Crowned with glory all their age.

Here's the bridge so well defended,
   Here Camillus beat the Gaul,
Here's where Clœlia won the shelter
   Of the sacred Roman wall.

But the Christian hero seeketh
   Christian consolation here,
For he looks to Him who healeth
   Every sorrow, every tear,—
And he dies, he dies an exile
   Far from green Tyrowen's hills:
Still his name, as once his war-cry,
   Many an Irish bosom thrills.

LINES

ON HEARING THOMAS DEVIN REILLY * DESCRIBE A VISIT TO
THE WICKLOW MOUNTAINS WITH HIS MOTHER.

THEY stood upon a Wicklow hill,
   A mother and her son,
Round them rise the heavenward mountains,
   By them bright the streamlets run;
Purple are the heath-flowers blooming,
   Green and golden is the sod,
And the blue above them shining
   Scarcely hides the throne of God.

Eastward lies the sea serenely,
   And their home is by its side,
And she prays on it a blessing,
   With a woman's love and pride.

---

* One of those who were forced to fly from Ireland in consequence of the
failure of the outbreak in '48.

But the boy—his heart is teeming
  Now with images sublime,
Freedom's ancient gospel fills him,
  Teachings of its olden time.

Mapped and chronicled before him,
  Lie proud Europe's battle-fields,
Martial music stirs and thrills him,
  Banners and the clash of shields.
But a cloud is calmly gathering
  On that young and noble brow,
And hot tear-drops seem to glisten,
  In the eyes that flashed e'en now.

For the land that lies before them,
  Bright in all the summer glow,
Hideth in its homes the sorrow
  Only Irish homes can know;
Beareth everywhere the branding
  Of its perjured master's hand,
In its graveyards, in its cities,
  In the mart, and on the strand.

And he vows to give his manhood,
  Heart and soul, and mind and will,
Erin's hapless homes with freedom,
  Comfort, peace, and love to fill.
Vowed and kept his vow, and perished
  In the blossom-time of life,
Exiled far from home and kindred
  In the immemorial strife.

ON SEEING AN OLD IRISHMAN BURST INTO TEARS WHILE
READING MITCHELL'S "LIFE OF HUGH O'NEIL."

THE old man casts the book aside, he cannot see for tears,
He cannot read the record of those disastrous years;
He cannot brook that Hugh O'Neil, his country's sword
    and shield,
Should perish otherwise than on an Irish battle-field.
He cannot choose but curse Mountjoy, a later scourge of
    God,
A modern Attila and more, who stained our natal sod
With blood of fellow-Christian men, who strove to shield
    and save
Their native homes and altars, for them all ills to brave.
He cannot choose but honor him, our own, our darling
    Hugh,
Whose dauntless heart and strong right hand so oft the
    foe o'erthrew.
He wanders back in thought to when from England's
    toils he came,
And Tullagh Oge beheld him crowned and worthy of
    his name.
He hails with brimming eyes once more the broad white
    banner spread
With the "Red Hand" of O'Neil, 'fore which the Saxons
    often fled.
Elizabeth and Cecil frown in dark and ruthless hate,
But Hugh has skill as deep as theirs, and heart with
    hope elate.
He trains his bands, he casts his balls, he brights his
    father's sword,
He strengthens old Dungannon, he wades the Yellow
    Ford,

He measures all Ulidia round as with a soldier's eye,
He knows, as if his childhood's home, each spot beneath
    its sky.
He takes unto his heart of hearts Tirconnel's glorious
    chief,
The young, the fiery, fearless Hugh (alas! those years,
    too brief).
He saves the shipwrecked Spaniards, and through them
    with their king
The ancient bonds of amity to closer ties would bring;
He brings the blessing Rome had sent, and for his holy
    faith
And for his fatherland goes forth, and to his people
    saith:
"This land is ours; a foreign Queen, an alien people
    claim
To rule Tirowen's fields as theirs, they brand our very
    name.
See Desmond lies in ashes; its priests are hunted, slain,
Its princes wait God's chosen time in old ancestral Spain.
But yesterday two sons of hers, from grave Alcala's halls
Which nursed their exiled youth, came forth, for now
    their country calls;
They sailed with that Armada so awfully o'erthrown,
And on their country's coast storm-cast, the princes died
    alone.
Munster is overmastered, my country-men, and we
Soon in our fathers' homesteads these faithless foes shall
    see.
But no! O'Neill forbids it, the spirit of our race
Arises in its grandeur, it calls to its embrace
All that remains of Erin, all that for her still live,
And faith and God and conscience a blessed presage
    give.

Now then Armagh is ours, Portmore shall be our own,
MacGuire of the Lakes shall see his cruel foes o'erthrown;
Downpatrick we shall guard it, our Saints within it lie,
MacGinnis shall have Down his own, from vale to moun-
    tain high;
We'll right thee, Ireland, now at last, or perish for thy
    sake.
Now men of ancient Erin, this solemn oath we take,
That, while our arms can aid, it, no English Queen shall
    sway
Our land, nor aught but Irish law shall Irishmen obey.
No novel creed shall here find room, no hireling preacher
    pray,
We hold the faith the Saviour taught, and bless it night
    and day."
Alas! alas! 'twas all in vain, the stranger won the fight,
And Ulster lost and Erin their glory and their light,
And the "two Hughs" as exiles laid down their weary
    lives.
O'Donnell in the bloom of life, while yet hope bravely
    strives,
In Spain, in proud Cimancas, he died, the young, the brave,
Who gave his land his life, his all, the faith to serve
    and save.
And Hugh O'Neil, worn out with years, laid down his
    weary crown
In the shadow of the Apennines, where Roman light
    streams down.
San Pietro, in Montorio—O Irish Pilgrim! stay
Your steps within its sacred walls, there weep awhile
    and pray,
For there lies Hugh O'Neil, the chief, who loved us to
    the last:
May God's eternal rest be his, now earthly woes are past!

TO MY ELDEST BROTHER.

AGAIN the spring is coming with its flowers
    And buds and leaves and thousand precious things,
Does it remind you, Willie, of the hours
    When our hearts had a buoyancy like spring's ?
Does it remind you how together often
    Thro' the green meadows we have rambled then,
For when the gales and showers began to soften
    They soon brought back the cowslip-bells again.

Does it remind you, Willie, of the currents
    That met and whirled away together there,
How in their beds we oft made mimic torrents
    That made sweet music in the summer air ?
Does it remind you how at sunrise waking
    We heard the happy birds that hailed with glee
The young, soft, trembling leaves so surely making
    Sweet sanctuaries for them of each green tree.

Do you not mind their nests in hidden places,
    Among the boughs or where the soft moss curled ?
In those bright days they almost knew our faces,
    And you would not have shot them for the world.
Do you remember that old ruined castle
    Where some proud Geraldine once held his state,
Home of the bard, the priest, the stalwart vassal,
    While Erin yet was struggling with her fate ?

Oh, from its walls how oft with gaze all eager
    Have we looked o'er the plains of rich Kildare,
Nor dreamed that e'er the false-hearted intriguer
    Had riveted his chains and fetters there ?

Our country seemed the paradise God made it,
 It looked all fair and free, and green and grand;
Oh little did we know how man betrayed it,
 How shame and sorrow sobbed thro' all the land!

That knowledge came our pride to grief all turning,
 He saw her, as she is, not as she seems,
And well I mind * the anger fierce and burning
 With which we cursed the Saxon and his schemes.
How many a futile plan we made to free her,
 How strong our hope the glorious day might be
When free and independent earth might see her,
 Her sons supreme from bounding sea to sea!

MY BROTHER'S ORDINATION.

At home! at home! where the old name awakens
 Memories and passions of the buried past,
There hath the Lord of Mercy called and signed thee
 To be his own, thou of our race the last.
At home! at home! in the ancestral chapel,
 Amid the shadows of our fathers there,
He chose thee for the temple, for the altar,
 While rose for thee full many a heartfelt prayer.

What are thy thoughts, my brother, lonely straying
 'Mong the green hills where we shall never rove;
Doth not a tall, proud shadow sometimes greet thee
 With the outpouring of a father's love?
Doth not the voice that soothed our earliest sorrows
 Cease for a while to mingle with the blest,
That it may pour into thy inmost bosom
 Words of beatitude and hope and rest?

* An idiom peculiar to the North of Ireland, or, rather, a provincialism.

Do not the faces, dear from earliest childhood,
   Gather around thee at the evening close?
Alas! between us the mysterious ocean
   Beareth its freight of exile and of woes.
Surging around us is the strong life breathing
   Its wild existence in this Western World,
While thou art there 'mid wreck and desolation,
   Thy home's hot ashes o'er thy pathway hurled.

Yet it is Erin, 'tis our home, our country,
   Our native land, our father's burial sod,
It is our blood and bone, our friends and kindred,
   For whom you offer up your life to God.
Around you stand the sacred hills that sheltered
   Our stout forefathers in the days of old,
Do you not feel their hot blood thrill and tingle?
   For Truagh's green woods their foemen have and hold.

Away beside the silvery Pacific   .
   Their name is honored and their sons are known,
And in this land of refuge, their descendants
   Are like the ocean's playthings cast alone.
Vengeance! my heart is hot, revenge is justice,
   Justice for mine and for my fathers' wrongs,
Pile it on Saxon heads! great God, uplift us,
   Arm us against their desolating throngs.

Fill us with strong and resolute endurance
   Might to resist and power to destroy
The rush of wrongs that stifle and consume us, .
   And turn our time-worn sorrow into joy.
Our race hath known no traitors, and we leave thee
   A hostage for our fealty evermore,
And we?—we vainly try to fix our future
   Lonely in some green nook of this strange shore.

ON AN ANCIENT COAT OF ARMS.

THE sea, what signifies it? the wild abounding sea
With the tall ship sailing stately before the breeze so
    free?
Ah, to us it tells a story, a tale of ancient days,
Of Heber and Heremon, and Amergin crowned with
    bays.
From Spain, from Spain, Milesius, in days renowned of
    old
He sailed with all his treasures of arms and men and gold;
They turned the brave ship westward, and the good God
    sped it well
Till it reached thy shore, green Erin, where the sunset
    shadows fell.

The moon so brightly gliding through dark and drifting
    clouds,
Before its radiance parting now, now closing in like
    shrouds;
It speaks of changeful fortunes, of shades that dim the
    light,
But yet of truest glory and a consummation bright.
Oh well, my stalwart fathers, full well you chose the
    queen
Of stars to tell your struggle long, within the island
    green.
For truly shadows oft have closed upon you dark and
    dread,
As when base Cromwell thought he'd laid your last son
    with the dead;
As when on old Drum Banagher its brave defender fell,
Against King William fighting, leading his clansmen well;

3

As when oppression ousted your sons from Truagh's
    green woods,
From Altha Diouhl's valley and Glass Lough's crystal
    floods.
But brightly as the moon beams your spirit sparkled still,
Still true to creed and country, with steadfast aim and
    will.
The stag and the bold wolf-dog in full and fleet career,
A tale they tell of pleasant sound to old tradition's ear,
How landing in the farthest South our first forefather,
    he
A hunting went with all his men and northward sped
    with glee.
No land along the Shannon, no land in Leinster broad
E'er stayed him, on and on he sped, though all the land
    was good.
But Truagh, green Truagh, it stayed him, it stayed his
    onward mood,
"And let us rest at last," he said, "within this pleasant
    wood,
For here shall be our home, and here a stronghold shall
    we build,
And after years shall see this land, with our descendants
    filled.
Oh sure a 'Happy Hunting,' * was this that brought us
    here,
And here my sons shall guard their own with battle-axe
    and spear;
But to the stranger coming a guest within your gate
For him a ready welcome there ever shall await,
From foemen they shall guard him with all their zeal
    and skill,
And safely shall they guide him beyond the reach of ill."

---

* *Fausta Venatio*, "Happy Hunting"—the motto that belongs to the Arms.

Oh surely when O'Donnell, Red Hugh, the brave and
    bold,
Escaped from Dublin castle in the stormy days of old,
Oh surely then, MacKenna, thy sons obeyed thee well,
They sheltered Erin's hero, they guarded him full well,
They left him in Tirconnell, a prince in princely state.
O Hugh, dear Hugh, like Erin's, how sorrowful thy fate!
O God, my God, shall never my country's sorrows cease,
Shall still her woes be endless, and change but to
    increase?
According to the multitude of thy great mercies, Lord,
Look down on her in mercy and peace shall be restored;
Say to that sea of sorrows, with all its waves, "Be still,"
And teach her children always to bless Thy holy will.

LINES

SUGGESTED BY THE ANCIENT HISTORY OF THE CONRYS,
IN THE ANNALS OF THE FOUR MASTERS.

I KNEW it, oh I knew it,
    That the Conry's spirit came
Of a glorious race and lineage,
    Noble in their every aim.

For I saw their stately bearing,
    And I knew their stainless hearts,
And I loved their loving natures,
    With a love naught else imparts.

Erst o'er Teffia's * hills and valleys
    They maintained a kingly sway,
Now its very name is altered,
    And the Conrys—where are they?

* Ancient name of Roscommon.

And in after days though olden
  O'Maol Conry placed the wand,
White and pure the type of justice,
  In the chief O'Connor's hand.

He proclaimed the chief's accession
  Sung his deeds, upheld his fame,
Bards and heroes all unnumbered
  Of thy race, O'Conry, came.

On Carn Fraoch * methinks I see them,
  Chieftain, Tanist, Brehon, Bard,
O'Maol Conry plights the monarch
  Connaught's laws and rights to guard.

Why have thy descendants wandered `
  Unregarded from the shore
Of the land their fathers sung of,
  Lost to Erin evermore ?

Ah! because their country's fallen,
  Lost her freedom, lost her lore,
Silent now the Bards of Erin,
  Ruthless strangers tread her shore.

Yet, my friends, thy name awakens
  In my bosom feelings deep,
Pride to learn thy fathers' glory,
  Grief and love that will not sleep.

----

* The mount where the O'Connor was inaugurated.

LINES WRITTEN AT THE CLOSE OF '48.

God of mercy, God of justice,
  Hear our prayer to-day!
Not for freedom, not for plenty,
  Not for peace we pray.

Self-abasement wrought our ruin,
  And we bend beneath the rod,
But the men who sought to save us,
  Save! O righteous God!

Oft in vain the blood of martyrs
  For our country had been poured,
Yet a hero band, to aid her,
  Sought to raise the avenging sword.

Sought to raise the Irish banner,
  Green and ancient like the Isle
Where for Faith's dear love, her people
  Suffer torture and exile.

Youth and genius and devotion
  Vainly, vainly did they give
To uplift their prostrate country,
  And to bid its sufferers live.

They had faith in right and justice,
  Hope in Irish strength and zeal,
Love for all the hopeless millions,
  Crushed beneath the despot's heel.

All in vain, for now our tyrants
  Hold them with remorseless hand,
And their blood, our friends, our brothers,
  Soon shall stain this hapless land.

But thy mighty hand, Creator!
  Soon can set the captives free.
Oh for help, for life, for justice,
  All thy people cry to thee!

MARIE ANTOINETTE.

Who is this, this queenly maiden,
  Peri-like and passing fair,
With that smile of proud affection,
  With those waves of radiant hair;
With those youthful years still ringing
  Through her memory, like sweet bells,
With that bearing, proudly, gentle,
  Of historic blood that tells?

From her native Danube flowing
  On through regions broad and fair,
From the proud Germanic nobles,
  And the homage paid her there,
Now she comes; for France hath wooed her
  With its weight of old renown,
And its youthful monarch offers
  At her feet his heart and crown.

Moves its chivalry to greet her,
  Knights and nobles, courtly dames,
And the Church's mitred princes,
  And the men of storied names,
And the wild, impulsive people
  Offer homage like to prayer,
While a thrill of rapture ringeth
  On the music-laden air.

Years flow on—she reigns supremely,
   Reigns the queen of every grace,
Art and nature's every beauty
   Find within her home a place.
She is Virtue's queen and Friendship's;
   Round that ancient Gallic throne,
With a wife's love and a mother's,
   She hath cast a golden zone.

But beneath it darkly heaving,
   What a dread volcano seethes,
What a world of angry passion
   Sendeth up its fiery wreaths!
And among the upturned faces
   Gazing on her from the crowd,
There are those who inly curse her,
   With a curse tho' deep not loud.

Curse her for their many sorrows,
   Sorrows not for her to heal,
Curse her for their dark oppression,
   For the load 'neath which they reel.
Ignorance hath been their portion,
   Bitter scorn, black want they know,
Led by demons, to the palace,
   Blind with loosened rage, they go.

Years flow on—oh spare me, spare me
   From the vision of those years!
Years of horror, years of anguish,
   Years of blood and hate and tears,
Years the darkest fate hath ever
   Sent to stain the ages yet,
For that maiden, queen and mother,
   Is Marie Antoinette.

Now a widow, worse than childless,
  Prisoned, tortured, and alone,
For her children, for her people
  She appeals to Mary's Son:
Prays within her cell so lonely,
  For her tyrant-foes take care
That nor priest nor pious sister
  Shall be with her in her prayer.

See her on that last dread journey,
  Wasted outcasts by her side,
Blanched the glossy hair, the aspect
  Old with sorrow, done with pride:
By her palace gates she passeth,
  By the stately Tuilleries,
By the Trianon, but never
  Rests one parting look on these.

But to dismal garret windows
  With a beaming, hopeful glance,
Full of heaven-inspired courage,
  Looks the martyr-queen of France.
There the priest of God is waiting,
  Filled with power from on high!
Thence he pours the absolution,
  Calmly now she goes to die.

From afar sweet home-wrought memories
  Flash upon her as of old,
But she flies to heaven for refuge.
  Soon the dismal tale is told;
For that stainless head falls stricken
  By the ruthless guillotine,
Drunk with blood, the murdress nation
  Slays its honor and its queen.

A LEGEND OF FLORENCE.

'Twas a fair chapel—piles of Parian marble,
    And rich mosaics, and sweet pictured saints,
And those bright frescoes where life seems immortal,
    Such as Corregio or as Titian paints,
Made it a shrine of beauty. O'er the altar
    Awfully beautiful, dead, crucified,
Hung the Redeemer, imaged, the heart broken
    Within the wound of that still bleeding side.
And yet no worshipper—the lamp of silver
    Costly and curious, hung as ever there,
But no light shone, no sign of adoration,
    Not the hushed presence of a creature's prayer.
Around reigned desolation—yet 'twas Florence,
    Haunt of the painter's heart, the poet's song;
Death and the plague in all its pleasant places,
    One dull, dread, silence thrilled its streets along.
My own fair Florence, in her summer splendor,
    Reeling in plague and laden with her dead,—
A horror grew upon me—all so lonely,
    Seeking for one I loved and would have wed.
Over the death-strewn city—through its columns,
    Marble and porphyry chased with sculptures rare,
Through aisles of gorgeous beauty and through places
    Where late abode the beautiful, the fair,—
I sought her. 'Twas a desert lone as Afric's,
    Fearfully quiet, terribly alone,
With its unpeopled palaces—sweet Florence!
    She seemed a queen struck dead upon her throne.
In the dear years scarce separate from childhood's,
    She showed me a fair chapel, umbrage-hid,
Where lay her buried mother and where ever
    She fled for refuge when tears came unbid.

3 *

I reached it—I was standing there this evening,
  My heart drawn onward to that altar lone,
It lay like earth within me—Was I dying?
  My very tears were leaden, cold as stone.
I could not kneel, nor cry, nor pray, nor prostrate,
  My life was stricken with too dread a woe,—
There was the very altar we had knelt at,
  That radiant girl and I, few moons ago.
On, on that altar called me—was the Presence,
  The eucharistic God-Head living there,
Mid the desertion waiting? Ah! I knew it,
  All my heart's agony ran o'er in prayer.
Still did that altar call me—blest Redeemer,
  Compassionate and merciful and good!
All, all is lost, but thee, sweet Lord, accept it,
  This broken heart in all its solitude!
Then the plague-thought oppressed me—"Oh! so lovely
  So young—so innocent—so soon to die—
And such a ghastly death—to lie unburied—
  God of my fathers! to thy feet I fly."
I tried to move, I reached at last the altar;
  On the white marble steps, her head laid down
On the rich crimson of the altar dais,
  Prostrate she lay—my Geraldine! my own!
Not mine, but thine, Lord Jesus! Thou hadst called her
  From out the plague-struck city to thy heart,
All had deserted thee in their wild terror,
  But she was true—her life was where Thou art.
And there she died in meekest adoration,
  No sign of grief on her sweet face, no tears
For friends too loved—no earthly passion
  Had ever wrecked her, with its joys and fears.
She lay there—deadly beautiful—her arm,
  All fair and young, pillowed her fairer cheek;
The deep blue veins made whiter the white forehead,

The lips scarce parted, seem'd as if they'd speak.
Dead and so pale,—the wavy silken tresses,
So chestnut-rich, and tinted all with gold,
Served for a coronet, thus fairly folded
Over that queenly brow so pure and cold.
Long robes of white were floating round her form,
She never looked so lovely until now.
O God! it was thy glorious Real Presence
That kept thy creature living through this woe,
That nerved my arms—while reverently and slowly
I bore thy chosen virgin to her grave,—
Her mother's grave,—and laid her in her bosom—
Then went *alone* the dread, dark world to brave.
But thou—my Peri, radiant, royal, lovely,
Thy lot was meet—gone in thy truth to God.
Blessed dear Lord! be this thy sweet election,
Only on me be laid the chastening rod.
Long years have passed since then—a very ocean
Of time and care hath swept across my heart,
The tale is like a legend, half-forgotten,
But buried thoughts to life will sometimes start.
Thus sometimes I remember thee and love thee,
My native Florence!—but for ever here
In the lone silence of my life thou dwellest,
Thou Angel of my path—*now doubly dear.*

TO FANNY.

Alas! what hopeless sorrow
Hath fallen upon this heart?
Its strings are steeped in sadness,
And hope doth not impart

Of all her rays of comfort,
  Of all her rays of peace,
One aid to still its throbbing
  Or bid its sorrow cease.

I saw thee grow beside me,
  A happy-hearted child,
With eyes of glee and gladness,
  And thoughts all undefiled;
And I longed with fruitless longing
  For the day that came too soon,
When years should bring thy sympathies
  Still nearer to my own.

It was not that I envied thee
  Thy young heart's careless joy,
Not that I sought to sadden thee
  With my own care's deep alloy;
But all friends were parted from me
  And I nursed my grief alone,
Lone as the desert pillar
  Of the gazer turned to stone.

And you seemed a heaven-sent soother
  Of a grief that grows not less,
With thy laugh's light joyous melody
  To soften and to bless—
To gather up the fragments
  Of a bruised and broken heart,
And gloss its deep rents over
  With affection's cherished art.

When man with arduous effort
  Hath changed a river's course,
It floweth on unseeming
  To hear the rude divorce;

But should the wintry tempest
  Come and choke the way they led,
Oh, with what headlong energy
  It seeks its early bed!

My feelings are that river,
  Thou leads't them o'er new ground,
But this all bitter parting
  Re-opens every wound.
It leaves me standing lonely,
  It snaps the binding chain,
And flings me back on memory
  And agony again.

There is a word whose sorrow
  Doth scorch the young heart up,
That fills to overflowing
  Affliction's bitter cup;
And we, alas! have said that word—
  But thou canst never tell,
What hordes of bitter memories
  Hang on that word, *farewell.*

JULIA.

MY beautiful sister Julia,
  Away in the dear old days
There was blessing and peace around thee,
  There was joy in thy gentle ways.
My darling, my own, my lovely,
  Young, beautiful poet-child,
With the light of grace like a halo
  Over that brow so mild.

My beautiful sister Julia,
  Away in the beautiful past
I picture thy face, my darling,
  With things too lovely to last.
I picture thee young and queenly,
  My mother's beautiful child,
The joy of that home, where beauty
  Of nature and art both smiled.

The golden curls, my darling,
  Again through my fingers twine,
And the soft dark eyes are speaking
  Of beautiful things to mine.
And the early flowers are gathered
  In festoons and garlands fair,
And the bird-songs are gladly thrilling
  The beautiful Irish air.

The lark from the rich red clover
  Rises and soars and sings,
I gaze till my eyes are dazzled
  As she whirls in luminous rings.
Beside me, my beautiful sister
  Filled with life's first young joy,
A child full of love and gladness,
  Love that knew no alloy.

Again, my beautiful sister,
  My darling, my love, my own,
I picture your face—a sorrow
  Over its sweetness thrown;
Chastened its bloom and softened,
  Hushed is thy silvery laugh—
Deep is the draught of sorrow
  Thy young lips learn to quaff.

Sad with an Irish sorrow
　I picture thy face, though now
The light of seventeen summers
　Gleams on thy queenly brow;
Beauty and grace and goodness,
　Purity, love, and truth,
And the love of thy God, together
　Richen thy beautiful youth.

A farewell comes back upon me,
　A parting too sad to name,
A rending away from Erin,
　And the life of an exile came.
Again, again, my darling,
　I picture your face as when,
In the weeds of an orphaned exile,
　You came to my heart again.

Death had bereft us wholly,
　Sisters and brothers dear—
The home-days had all departed,
　Life like a "famine year."
O Julia, my sweet young sister,
　My beautiful poet-child!
Sweetly and calm your spirit
　Clung to the cross and smiled.

Clung to the cross of Jesus,
　Chose to be his alone,
Left us for his love, my darling,
　My sister, my child, mine own.
Again, my beautiful sister,
　I picture thy pale, sweet face:
The Bride of the Lamb, how meekly
　She takes in his house her place!

The veil falls darkly round her
  To shut the cold world away,
And now "Sister Mary Francis"
  Lives but to love and pray.
And now, my heart's own sister,
  Bound by the same dear vows,
We'll work for the poor of Jesus,
  We'll serve the same glorious Spouse.

But the tears come back, my darling,
  Sorrow was never far,
In the midst of her work she faded,
  Set, like a pale sweet star—
Life ebbed in whirling eddies,
  Death had come down and closed
Those beautiful eyes where mercy
  · And God's holy love reposed.

QUÆ EST ISTA?

Quæ est ista? O my Saviour!
  'Tis a question sad to hear,
And it thrills through all my being
  With a feeling like to fear.
Quæ est ista? Not a maiden
  In baptismal whiteness now,
Comes to bear its precious emblem
  O'er a fair and frownless brow.

But a brand from out the burning
  Snatched by Thine all-potent hand,
Or a wretch from drowning rescued,
  Brought to life and brought to land.

Quæ est ista? Ah! Lord Jesus,
It is I,—Thou knowest well
What a sea of sorrow o'er me
At these little words doth swell.

It is I—O Lord, for ever
Let these words as now but speak
Of abasement and contrition,
Of a heart that fain would break!
Fain would break, but that Thy mercy
Binds as with the bonds of love:
The bruised reed Thou will not trample
Nor the broken heart reprove.

Quæ est ista? O Lord Jesus!
One who would be all Thine own,
Who o'er nature's broken forces
Fain would raise for Thee a throne:
Would be like Thee, would be near Thee,
Sitting humbly at Thy feet,
There to hear Thy words of mercy,
There imbibe Thy spirit sweet.

Would be like Thee?—but, O Jesus!
Who shall e'er be like to Thee,
Like Thee, Saviour of the nations?
Yet Thou sayest, "Learn of Me!"
To be like Thee in Thy mercy,
Like Thee in Thy humbleness,
Like Thee, silent in injustice,
Like Thee, patient in distress!

I remember, I remember,
In the sunny days gone by,
How I heard Thee sweetly call me,
Yet I madly sought to fly,

Clung with fearless, fast affection
  To the few that held my heart;
But Thy strong right hand hath rent us
  With resistless force apart.

O my Saviour, shield and save them,
  Bless them newly every day,
For they love Thee and they serve Thee,
  Be their comfort, be their stay!
It is true, dear Lord, I love them,
  But Thou lov'st them better still,
If it break my heart to leave them—
  Let it break, but do Thy will.

Now at last I come to seek Thee,
  Come to love Thee, come to serve
Thee among Thy chosen children,
  Never more from Thee to swerve.
Mary, Queen of peace and mercy,
  Give me strength against thy foes!
Help me, pity me, my Mother,
  For thou knowest all my woes!

"HE WHO COMETH TO ME, I WILL NOT CAST OUT."

JESUS, Son of God, and Saviour of the thankless race of
    men!
Jesus merciful and patient! Jesus, speak those words
    again!
Let me hear them, my Redeemer, down within my sad
    heart's deep,
Where affection, pained and anxious, seeks from all con-
    trol to leap.

Let me hear them, faint and fainter grows my hope to
come to Thee
Till I hear them—then exulting, over deserts lone I flee—
Over deserts lone and cheerless, where I miss each long-
loved face,
Then they gladden into regions lit with glory and with
grace.

Let me hear them, years of sorrow, years of wasted love
and truth
Toll strange knells through memory's chambers, years of
lost and squandered youth;
Dim life's old hope, dim and cheerless, baseless all the
trust and vain,
So long placed in human friendship, human pleasure,
human pain.
She who comes to Thee, my Saviour! oh Thou wilt not
cast her off,
Not though she has erred and wandered, wronged Thee
worse than those that scoff
At Thy light, because they know not of Thy works and
ways and will,
For at ruined, broken cisterns they, alas! their pitchers
fill.

Jesus, Babe and Boy and Teacher! Jesus, weary by the well,
Waiting in Thy mercy's patience, words of healing hope
to tell;
Jesus, Son of David, Jesus humble, sorrowful and lone!
By the world you came to die for, all unthought of and
unknown;
Jesus, Son of Mary, Jesus, King of kings and Lord of
lords!
Jesus, at whose word the powers wave their arch-
angelic swords!

O Lord Jesus, God and Saviour! Thou art *there* our own,
    our own,
Heaven is surely there, for Thou art there, upon Thy
    mercy's throne.
There upon that lowly altar, 'neath those frail and
    simple veils,
Oh, to serve Thee and to love Thee till the life Thou
    gavest me fails!
"She who comes to me, I will not that she may rejected
    be—"
O Lord Jesus! I am coming—coming *after all* to Thee.

IN ANSWER TO A DEAR FRIEND.

THE leaves, the leaves, their gentle sway is ending,
    Soon like the summer shall they pass away;
And radiant tints of gold and crimson blending
    Shall herald and enlighten their decay.
Then shall the "four o'clocks" be all departed,
    Various and bright although their colors be,
No lesson shall they speak to the sad-hearted,
    Drawn from their lives so lovingly by thee.

The "morning glory" with its early splendor
    Shall leave no relic of its proudest bloom;
Like human hopes, the loving and the tender,
    Low shall it lie in time's corroding tomb.
But Fancy's flowers shall flourish, we shall cull them,
    We three together, many a frosty eve;
Cold criticism's scorn shall not annul them,
    Nor at its fiat shall we have to grieve.

Long shall our journeys be o'er earth and ocean,
    You with your "muse" shall lead to "Erin Green,"
Julia shall there be all at home, emotion
    Choking her heart for her discrownèd queen.

But let us travel on, let Jordan's waters
  Bring music to our ears, refresh our feet;
And let us list the song of Juda's daughters,
  Soft in the twilight, silvery and sweet.

Let us see Bethlehem, so lone, so dreary,
  Unless faith fills it with its loving light;
Let us bow down our spirits so earth-weary,
  'Tis our Creator, veiled from human sight.
Why to the sombre garden that looks over
  Jerusalem's doomed streets, may we not fly,
While angels sorrow-stricken o'er it hover,
  There where the Son of God prepares to die?

Calvary is near, and all around are traces,
  Footsteps of Him, obedient unto death,
Death such as scares the heart—oh what effaces
  Its memory from us till our parting breath?
Calvary is near, but not afar is Thabor,
  Glory is on its summit and around:
So from this life of sorrow and of labor
  Pass we to life with bliss immortal crowned.

A DREAM.

'Twas evening at Saint Catharine's,
  The sun was sinking slow,
And the solemn choir was lighted
  By its faint and fading glow.

Thoughtful Novice, vowed Religious,
  Bowed in reverence divine,
They were kneeling near to Jesus,
  They were kneeling near his shrine.

Each one hears her own heart's whisper,
  Each one reads her own life's tale;
Happy Novice, vowed Religious,
  Each in thoughtfulness grows pale.

There is silence—sacred silence—
  Soundless worship breathes around,
Adoration hushed and humble,
  Self-abasement, mute, profound.

Now the soft air thrills, the music
  Of a human voice is heard;
And my inmost heart, it acheth,
  All responsive to her word.

Young she seems and fair and stately,
  With a queenly look and tone,
Gently firm to bear and suffer
  Life's strange mystery alone.

Thoughtful still for others' sorrow,
  Sympathetic, and *so true*,
Motherlike, care's twisted meshes
  Sweetly anxious to undo.

But she speaks, my full heart bids me
  See the face I love so well,
And I listen all soul-stricken,
  Bound as by some mystic spell.

Now her eyes are turned upon me,
  Quiet eyes, so thoughtful deep;
While I think of them, there's something
  Makes me sad enough to weep.

And she speaks to me: "Remember,
  Not by strange and sudden flights
Is the heart brought near to Jesus,
  Does it come to his delights.

"Not poetic fits of praying,
  Not enthusiastic love,
Living through few fleeting hours,
  Ever reached a home above.

"Love is active, love endureth,
  Labors long and labors late,
Love is suffering, love rejoices
  In the cross with heart elate;

"Love is humble, love is lowly
  Love is trustful, love is strong,
Love can sacrifice its treasures,
  Live a life alone and long.

"Love is constant—love consumeth
  All that self had ever prized,
Gives its life-blood, the libation
  Of a thing disdained, despised;

"Little worth, for love discerneth
  Tremblingly the Infinite,
And bows down abashed and silent—
  Offering thus the 'widow's mite.'"

Words like these, methought I heard them
  In that voice and tone of hers,
Which for ever all my being
  Strangely wins and strangely stirs.

But I woke—I was but dreaming
And the aching heart within
Whispered faintly "Mother Agnes,
When shall I to love begin?"

But no sweet voice answered kindly.
I am here * alone, alone,
Hide me, hide me, O my Saviour!
In the shadows of Thy throne.

Help me in the coming sorrows,
   Thou art taking from the earth
One† who lit my life's sad pathway
   Since the fête-day of her birth.

One, my child, my friend, my sister,
   Meek and humble, pure of heart;
She is Thine, dear Lord, but keep us
   Not eternally apart.

Never let created shadows
   Come between her soul and mine,
But let both be laid as victims,
   Self-devoted, on Thy shrine.

LINES

ADDRESSED TO THE LATE MOST REV. ARCHBISHOP HUGHES,
ON THE TENTH CELEBRATION OF THE FEAST OF OUR
LADY OF MERCY, IN THE CONVENT OF MERCY, N. Y.

FAR in the light of heaven, within the Sacred Heart
Sweet mercy reigns and triumphs, of Jesus' life a part;

---

* Written at the Convent of Mercy, Greenbush, N. Y.
† Sister M. Francis.

Its home is there, its essence, and all its wealth of love,
And justice reigns beside it, an equal claim to prove.
But in the heart of Mary, our Mother and our Queen,
It reigns without a rival, all peaceful and serene.

Over the earth's green bosom she turned her pitying eyes,
And saw its purchased people their Savior's blood despise;
Here 'mid this new-world splendor, where nature revels
    wild,
She saw its dazzling vesture with dark sin-stains defiled;
She saw where Faith was wanting. where it was worn
    and wan,
Where Charity was dying and Hope strove on alone.

Perhaps the thought, sweet Mother, of that long by-
    gone day,
When for this land Columbus knelt down to her to
    pray;
And as she thought, that "Salve" again came streaming
    o'er
The dreamy blue of heaven, across its starry floor.
And then his dedication of all this glorious land,—
Did it not claim redemption and mercy at her hand?

And then, Most Reverend Father, she turned her eyes on
    you,
She touched your heart and told you the work you were
    to do;
She pointed o'er the ocean to that old martyr isle
Where, 'neath their priceless burden, cross-laden Chris-
    tians smile,
Smile and unto their bosoms that blood-stained standard
    press,
Rich in their want and lofty in all their humbleness.

4

She pointed out her children, the agents of her love,
Mercy is theirs, she brought them its spirit from above.
Oh 'tis but ten years, Father most honored, most revered,
Since then with you the Sisters here mercy's stronghold
    reared—
But ten years! yet the seedling has grown a goodly tree,
And like a tree is spreading its branches fast and free.

Branches that, like the banyan's, still keep their long-
    loved hold   ·
On this, their mother-homestead, where first they joined
    the fold ;
Far in the West our Sisters have founded mercy's shrine,
And raised its spotless banner 'round which all virtues
    twine.
There the poor child of labor, neglected or despised,
Will learn the way to heaven, her spirit's worth is prized.

Besides us, dear Saint Francis,* to whom his God was *all*,
Has found our Sisters ready to hear his thrilling call,
Like him to serve our Savior, like him to bear the cross,
Like him to love the spirit that counts earth's gold as
    dross.
They, too, will ever cherish Archbishop Hughes's name—
Has not their well loved mother † on him a special claim?

Far o'er the sea's strange waters, in youth's bright day
    she came,
With you for love of Jesus, and in His Sacred Name,

---

* In allusion to the foundation of St. Francis's Convent of Mercy, Brooklyn,
L. I., whose first Mother-Superior came out with the Sisters whom Archbishop Hughes brought from Ireland in 1846.

† Mother Mary Agnes O'Connor, first Mother-Superior of the Convent of
Mercy, N. Y.

Our own dear Mother Agnes—it needs no words to tell
With what a tide of feeling her heart this day must swell;
And while she thanks her Savior for all his light and aid,
She blesses our sweet Mother, who for it oft had prayed.

She blesses with her children their father and their
    friend,
And prays the peace of heaven upon him to descend,
She blesses God who called her from country and from
    home,
To save the wandering exile, doomed friendless else to
    roam,
To raise a shrine of mercy, a refuge for the poor,
Where they can peace and pardon, and grace and life
    insure.

From Truagh's green woods far roaming, from Bragan's
    mountain lone,*
From Altha-Diaoul's valley where stands "St. Patrick's
    Stone,"†
From all old Erin's homesteads we find them struggling
    here,—
What blessedness to keep them, their Savior's bosom
    near!
That bliss is thine; in heaven may it your crown
    increase
With gems of star-like lustre, when this poor life shall
    cease!

* "The Green Woods of Truagh" and Bragan Mountain are named as being near the Archbishop's birthplace.
† In the valley of Altha-Diaoul there is a famous stone, formerly a Druid's Altar. St. Patrick, according to the legend, blessed it, and immediately a large hollow which it contained was filled with water, which the Saint used to baptize the multitude of converts present.

ON A DEATH'S HEAD.

AWFUL face so dry and bare,
Gazing on me eyeless there,
Remnant of a human life,
Sharer in its parting strife,
Dreadful witness from the tomb,—
What wert thou in life's young bloom?
Wert thou native in land,
Born among its forests grand?
Did its giant rivers lave
Thy young limbs so fleetly brave,
Did the freedom it had won
Make thee proud to be its son?
Exile wert thou, half alone
Though 'mong crowds familiar grown,
Thinking of thy native skies,
Where Italia, song-loved, lies,
Mourning over Poland's fate,
Or for France, the fair, elate?
Wert thou born among the hills,
Where the Irish nature thrills,
Did'st thou come from leafy isles
Where undying summer smiles?
What avails it—thou art dead,
All life's golden sands have sped.
Still thou gazest— *still* I ask,
What was thy life's given task,
What wert thou, when life and love,
Made thy heart so joyous move?
Did the storm of passion sweep,
Thy soul as storm-winds the deep?

Wert thou humble, patient, true,
Keeping life's great end in view ?
Did'st thou bear a broken heart,
Wert thou wed to love and art;
Wert thou fair to look upon,
Wert thou poet, priest, or nun ?
Awful presence, what wert thou,
Thy spirit where abides it now;
Hast thou fought a holy fight,
Livest thou in realms of light;
Art thou near to Jesus' feet,
Dost thou hear his pleading sweet,
For us, whom he loved and saved,
Death and all its terrors braved ?
Dost thou see his wounds divine,
In the heaven like suns that shine ?
Soul—oh say it!—art thou lost,
On a fiery ocean tossed ?
Did'st thou sell thy soul for sin,
Doth each day thy woes begin ?
Wretched soul, thou hast not known
God's sweet love around thee thrown,
Perhaps thy first dark evil day
To Eternity gave way!
But I have sinned and sinned for years,
Wherefore flow, ye bitter tears;
Flow ye on, like lava, flow,
Burn out all this deadly woe;
Flow ye on, like Lethè, fast
O'er the agonizing past;
Flow ye on, like Jordan's tide,
Near which Jesus lived and died,
Flow ye on till death's last sighs,
And they close,—those weary eyes!

STAY WITH US, LORD!

STAY with us, Lord, our feet are very weary,
   The golden sunset dies among the hills;
Stay with us, Lord, life's night is cold and dreary,
   It comes with all its dew-damps and its chills.

Shall it be night star-gemmed and borealised,
   Waving for banner the wide milky way,
Night in its halls sidereal proudly palaced,
   Out-queening all the glory of the day?

Or night with tempest shaken and with thunder,
   Or gloomy with cold rain and desert wind;
Night with no stars, its rolling cloud-mass under,
   No gleam from the lost day left far behind ?

Night, when the weary heart knows no reposing,
   Night, when the o'erwrought brain throbs fierce and
      wild,
Night, when rich memory's curtains keep unclosing,
   Till age sheds tears that might beseem a child ?

Or peaceful night when no earth-vapors darken,
   When the free soul is lifted to its Lord,
And the rapt spirit blissfully may hearken,
   In the deep silence, to his glorious word ?

Stay with us, Lord, we have no hope but in thee,
   No light, no love, no rest but at thy feet;
Stay with us, Lord, our sick hearts long to win thee
   To be our guest—with thee even death is sweet.

QUOTH THE ANGEL, "EVERMORE."

ANGEL, who hast guarded ever
   This wild life from falling o'er
The dark precipice it stands on,
   Shall it stand there evermore ?
   Quoth the Angel, "Evermore."

Shall the love that grew in beauty
   Far on childhood's daisied floor,
Live in spite of·years and sorrows,
   Love what time can ne'er restore ?
   Quoth the Angel, "Evermore."

Evermore shall I the places
   Empty in my heart deplore ?
Seeking ever missing faces,
   Pining for my natal shore,
   Fever-hearted evermore ?

Evermore shall voices haunt me,
   When the night-rains wildly pour,
Like life passionately rushing
   To Eternity's dread shore ?
   "Thou shalt hear them evermore."

Golden curls and long dark lashes,
   Cast like shadows softly o'er
Eyes of sad but loving lustre,
   Shall I see them nevermore ?
   Quoth the Angel, "Nevermore."

Nevermore, a black veil floateth
   Where the gold curls hung of yore,
And beneath it death unceasing
   Saps life's pulses evermore—
   Ever, ever, evermore!

Angel! angel! bear to heaven
Gloriously my sister-child,
She was mine through years of anguish,
Held my heart with sorrow wild,
She, all sinless, undefiled.

Angel, shall I ever, ever
Reach the goal to which she'll soar?
Are they lost, all lost, forever?
Shall I meet them nevermore?
Death—will it the loved restore?

Empty day-dreams, shall they ever
Cheat me, heavenward as they soar?
Dead-Sea fruits, all filled with ashes,
Shall I eat them evermore?
Quoth the Angel, "Evermore,

Shall I drink the cup I poisoned
At a fount that flows no more,
Till it freeze the heart that filled it,
And "life's fever" all is o'er?
Quoth the Angel, "Evermore—

"Evermore till deaths unnumbered
Shall exhaust wild passion's store,
Till its pride is quenched as ashes,
Till its pulse shall throb no more,
Dying daily evermore."

MAGDALEN.

St. Magdalen, the beautiful, the glorious,
Lovely as life, when life is in its spring,
We may not stem the floods that sweep thy spirit,
Nor loose the arms thus to the cross that cling.

We may not see thee with thy long hair falling,
  Like a deep veil of sorrow o'er thy form,
Thy dark Judean eyes subdued and saddened,
  Thy proud head bent 'neath sorrow's thunder-storm.

We may not see thee at the feet of Jesus,
  While fall those showers of priceless, wordless tears,
We may not hear that voice divinely tender,
  That healed thy heart and softened all thy fears.

We cannot feel how infinitely blessed
  That heart of thine grew in that wondrous hour,
Streams of sweet love, divine and pure and holy,
  Dyed it, as sun-rays dye an opening flower.

Love overmastered love—the love of Jesus
  For ever quenched the love that lives of earth,
Not by slow steps and dull degrees, but brightly
  Sprung to existence in its hour of birth.

It seized on all the powers of thy being,
  Made thy heart hot with new and nameless life,
Thy mind a volume where His name was written,
  Existence, sacrifice, with triumph rife.

Love! love! O Magdalen, I die with envy,
  He did not save thee as He saved my soul,
Thy unbaptized iniquities were shadows
  To those whose phantoms through my memory roll.

And yet thy love is strong as death, while mine is
  One half imagination and deceit,
Flowers with no fruit, a summer with no autumn,
  A poet's dream, a half-discovered cheat.

But thou with thy great soul that knew no quailing,
  Thy passionate young heart broke, and for Him,
Thy sunny beauty shattered in thy sorrow,
  Thine eyes dark tenderness grown dull and dim.

Oh, thou art love's best trophy, its best emblem—
    Standing where stands the Mother, by the cross,
Gazing upon it, drinking in His sorrow,
    Breathing the agony, the pain of loss—

The *loss of Jesus*, of His loving presence,
    Of the sweet light of his forgiving eyes,
The sound of that blest voice, whose every accent
    Called thee on nearer, nearer to the skies.

Now He has gone—the light hath all departed,
    The life that was *thy* life hath left thee lone,
No word to cheer thee on, no look of mercy,
    Darkness around thee as a pall is thrown.

Earth is a waste all flowerless and frozen,
    Life a long exile—drearier each day;
There are no floods of bright tears, all unbidden,
    Weeping the bitterness of grief away.

There seems to be *no Jesus*, clouds and vapors,
    And the night-skies, starless and grey and cold,
Gather between thy earth-home and His heaven,
    Till thy heart freezes with a woe untold.

We may not see thee in thy lone seclusion
    To be in all things his thy only care,
To know no knowledge but the name of Jesus,
    To be like Him, thy passion and thy prayer.

We, with our dull eyes, cannot read the lessons
    The Heart of Jesus taught thee when at last
Nearer He drew thee home—home to thy centre:
    Dear Magdalen, the trial hour is past.

'Tis past! that night of dull unspoken anguish,
    Again the sun-rays stream, the flowers ope,
If it is night, 'tis night with all its splendors,
    Star-gemmed and glorious, bright with love and hope.

O Magdalen! the darkness has departed,
　And life goes with it; now that beating heart
Breaks all its bonds and rushes to its centre—
　Prostrate at Jesus' feet once more thou art.

St. Magdalen the well-beloved of Jesus,
　His trophy purchased by His Sacred Blood,
Pray that the grace He died to pour upon us,
　May cleanse our hearts in that all-saving flood!

JESUS IN PRISON.

"I saw Him lean for an instant against the pillar, surrounded with light."
—"SUFFERINGS OF CHRIST."

I saw Him in the dungeon,
　'Twas a dark and rugged cell,
Horrors gathered quickly round Him,
　As the sea-waves crowd and swell,
While they break in torrents o'er Him,
　'Whelmed within their dread eclipse;
Love of us illumes the darkness,
　Moves in pardoning prayer His lips.

All that radiant hair is torn,
　All that face with filth defiled,
Blood-shot are those eyes where mercy
　Made her home in lustre mild.
Those blest hands,—the hands of Jesus,
　That within them healing bore,
They are bound and bruised and bleeding,
　Bleeding now at every pore!

Ah those blessed hands! but see them
　As an infant's rosy, fair,
Playing with the lily-blossoms,
　Smoothing Mary's folded hair;

See them, even there uplifted
　To the throne of grace above,
For the race He was to rescue
　With such unrequited love.

Now He leans against the pillar
　In the damp chill gloom of night,
Lo! from heaven there streams a radiance
　With divinest glory bright.
In that mystic light transfigured,
　Jesus! we adore Thee now,
Though the robe of scorn is round thee,
　And its crown is on Thy brow.

All that blood and filth and torture
　In its light like jewels gleam,
Cherubim and seraph, near Him,
　As ignoble creatures seem.
Over earth and sea He gazeth
　With an omnipresent eye,
On the myriad host of sinners
　For whose sake He deigned to die.

Into years, 'mid far off ages,
　Into regions then unknown,
On the hearts that here adore Him,
　And He chose them for His own;
Stretched out then His burdened arms
　To accept their load of sin,
And to draw them close and closer
　That mysterious light within.

Now the time is come, Redeemer,
　Make them worthy to be Thine,
Make them do the things that please Thee,
　Fill them with Thy love divine;

Teach them how to love and suffer,
   How to close the spirit's eyes
To this passing world, that nearer,
   Closer to Thee, it may rise!

Earth is dark to me, my Saviour,
   Ah! Thou knowest what they bear,
Whom Thou gavest me to cherish
   And to love while mine they were.
But those days are past—Redeemer,
   Saviour, Jesus!—be their all,
Their resource, their strength, their comfort,
   Hear them, for on Thee they call.

BENEDICAMUS DOMINO.

LET us bless the Lord, dear Sisters,
   Let us bless our gracious Lord,
Let us praise Him, let us bless Him,
   Let us love His holy word.

Let us bless Him for the woodlands,
   For the sun and for the shade,
For the myriad joyous creatures
   That for us His mercy made.

Let us bless Him for St. Xavier's, *
   Where the city's ceaseless cry
Is unheard, and we are gazing
   On the pure, unshadowed sky—

Where in strangers we meet sisters,
   Sisters, in affection true,
Sisters, linked in love of Jesus,
   Sisters, with one goal in view.

* St. Xavier's Convent of Mercy, Latrobe, Pa.

Let us bless Him that He brought us
    Here together at His feet,
Let us pray that each may serve Him,
Till in heavenly bliss we meet.

Let us bless Him, our Redeemer,
    Let us love His Sacred Heart,
Prayer and penance let us offer
    In its praise, with love's sweet art.

Let us bless the Heart of Jesus,
    Let us bless our Lord who made
For our weary hearts a shelter
    In the tabernacle's shade.

Let us bless Him—He hath chosen
    These poor hearts to be His own,
Let us lay them sorrow-broken
    On the footsteps of His throne.

Let us bless Him—He hath bound us
    By the bonds of love and grace,
And by vow and veil and promise,
    Till we see Him face to face.

Let us bless Him—He hath called us
    From amid life's flowery ways,
All its rosy curtains opened,
    Placed the truth before the gaze.

Cast His light upon the landscape,
    Showed the thorns its roses hid,
And our long delays how gently—
    Oh, how gently He hath chid!

Let us bless Him—He hath loved us,
    Made our lot the choicest, *best*,
Made our sorrows His compassion,
    We are His and we are blest.

Let us bless Him,—down from heaven
  To the lowliness of earth
He descended, the Eternal!
  And among us had His birth.

Let us bless Him as an infant
  Sleeping on His mother's breast;
Let us listen, she is singing
  The Creator to His rest.

Let us bless Him, the Lord Jesus,
  As He grows in age and grace;
He the splendor of the Father,
  Let us kiss His footstep's trace.

Let us hasten—He hath called us
  To pursue His chosen path;
Deeds of mercy, love, and meekness,
  Are the mile-stones that it hath.

Let us listen, He has said it,
  "Take thy cross and follow Me,"
Mortify weak nature's fancies,
  Burst its fetters and be free.

Let us hasten, O Lord Jesus!
  Calvary may not be far,
When the darkness comes, my Saviour,
  Oh, be Thou our polar star!

ELLA'S TWENTY-FIRST BIRTH-DAY.

ANOTHER wasted year,
        Ella dear,
Wasted in wayward hope and wayward fear,
        Ella dear;

Another year gone o'er
To that mysterious shore
Where partings are no more,
                    Ella dear.

A grave thought—"twenty-one,"
                    Ella dear,
So many joys and sorrows early gone,
                    Ella dear;
Twenty-one changeful years,
With all their fruitless tears,
Their bridals and their biers,
                    Ella dear.

Life bears an aspect new,
                    Ella dear,
One nearer to the real and the true,
                    Ella dear;
Now choose the better part,
Now free thy mind and heart,
Now learn love's sacred art,
                    Ella dear.

Ella, my own, my lost,
                    Ella dear,
Vainly life wastes in sorrow, storm-tossed,
                    Ella dear;
Ella, my eldest, mine,
No longer idly pine,
Master that will of thine,
                    Ella dear.

Ella, my eldest child,
                    Ella dear,
Ne'er from my heart, tho' from my home, exiled,
                    Hope and fear

Both keep me near you still,
In spirit and in will,
Though cares my bosom fill,
            Ella dear.

TO A NOVICE.

BLESSED St. Aloysius,
    Faithful to every grace,   .
Pray that our dear young sister
    May all your steps retrace;
May tread the path that led you
    So early to our Lord,
May be like you, all sinless,
    In thought and deed and word.

Like you, life's dearest treasures
    She left for His dear love,
Like you, she freely gave all
    To gain a home above.
Then let no fond affection,
    No passing joy or care
Be to her peace a poison,
    Be in her path a snare.

The care to be like Jesus,
    Humble and meek of heart;
The love His will to cherish,
    Let this be her sole art.
And may my loved young sister,
    My own dear novice-child,
Be every day more Christ-like,
    More gentle, patient, mild.

BIENTOT.*

Soon, soon return, sweet hopes so early vanished,
  Soon, soon return, dear day-dreams of my heart;
Soon, soon return, life's early aspirations—
  What fiat dread hath said to ye, "depart"?

Soon, soon return, young joy, with that sweet chalice
  Of which I quaffed so early and so deep—
Return, return, my inmost heart is aching,
  It thirsts for thee when weary eyes would sleep.

Return, return, my young appreciation
  Of all the beautiful, the good, the true,
My blissful ignorance of human baseness,
  And the glad future that seemed half in view.

"Soon, soon return?"—Alas how vain! how fruitless,
  This passionate appeal, this loud heart-call;
The past is dead, it cannot know returning,
  Why doth it hold my spirit in its thrall?

"Soon, soon return?"—Alas! alas! can sorrow
  Return with all its gloomy hues and dyes,
While joy returns not, till the soul that seeks it
  Back to the source of being soars and flies?

"Soon soon return?"—No, there is no returning,
  Earth hath no truthfulness, no changeless love;
Vainly the heart may seek its rest in creatures,
  'Tis made for God, for His bright home above.

"Bientot"—oh soon, soon, soon, my wondrous Ella,
  So little known and yet so strangely dear;
Soon may God's love lift off this weight of sorrow,
  And thy soul rise into its native sphere.

* These lines were suggested by hearing a young lady murmur frequently in sleep the word *bientot*.

Not within convent walls alone, dear Ella,
  May peace and hope and truest love be found;
The world is His, the heart may be a cloister,
  A fountain sealed, where most its joys abound.

Soon, soon may thine be such; may God's best blessing
  Begem thy path and gild it with His light,
That, when time's weary years have closed, thy spirit
  And mine may meet beyond the bounds of night.

Farewell, my strange, sweet Ella—very often
  My thoughts in prayer shall pause upon thy name,
To beg that soon the peace of Christ may bless thee,
  And that our place in heaven may be the same.

"I HAVE GONE ASTRAY LIKE A SHEEP THAT IS LOST—SEEK THY SERVANT."*

SEEK Thy child, Lord Jesus,
  Call Thy wanderer home;
Lone o'er thorny pathways
  Wild her footsteps roam.

Seek Thy child, life-wearied
  After twenty years;
See, her heart is bleeding—
  Dry her burning tears.

Seek Thy servant—save her,
  Jesus, God of peace,
God of all compassion,
  Let this long strife cease!

* Note.—The young girl for whom these lines were written, died broken-hearted, in her 21st year.

Bruised her feet and weary,
  Weary with the way,
Seek Thy child, Lord Jesus,
  Wandering thus astray.

The bruisèd reed, my Saviour,
  Thou wilt never break;
This crushed heart in mercy
  To Thy bosom take.

Take this broken flower,
  Winter came too soon;
Clouds shut out the sunlight
  Even in life's noon.

Take this broken flower,
  Press it to Thy heart,
Tinge its faded petals
  With Thy love's sweet art.

Free the bird long prisoned,
  Brokenly its wings
Beat against the fetters
  Time around it flings.

Wild its heart-pulsations,
  Faint its low death-song,
Lone its lingering hours,
  Brief, and yet how long!

Grace hath sovereign power,
  True love is divine;
Jesus, God of mercy,
  Make thy creature thine.

Thine at last, Lord Jesus,
These wild twenty years,
Washed out in Thy life-blood,
Purified in tears.

All their woes and sorrows
Quiet at Thy feet,
Where her heart lies bleeding,
Yet with peace replete.

All her future gilded
With Thy saving grace,
All her joy to love Thee,
And to see Thy face.

FOR THE CONFRATERNITY OF THE SACRED HEART.

O SACRED Heart, we come to Thee in sorrow,
O Sacred Heart, we come to Thee in love,
O Sacred Heart, our refuge, our asylum,
Our hope on earth, our joy in heaven above!

O Sacred Heart, we come to Thee in sorrow,—
Sorrow, for we have sinned, forgetting Thee;
We come to Thee in sorrow, Heart of Jesus,
Oh burst the bonds of sin and set us free!

O Sacred Heart, Thy children long to love Thee,
To lay their best affections on Thy shrine;
They long to serve Thee faithfully and truly—
O Heart of Jesus, make them wholly Thine.

O Sacred Heart, our refuge, our asylum,
  We fly to thee for hope, for rest, for peace;
Sweet Heart of Jesus, loving Heart of Jesus,
  Save Thy poor children, let their sorrows cease!

O Sacred Heart, our joy in God's bright heaven,
  Lead us Thyself along the narrow way;
Ah, dearest Lord, refresh us, we are weary,
  And at Thy feet our burden fain would lay!

THE NATIVITY.

She kneels in prayer, a solemn darkness round her
  Shadows her quiet beauty, for the night
Veils all its constellations, earth lies hidden
  As ere God's love had blest it into light—
She kneels in prayer, the world's cold, thoughtless scorn
  Has just been poured upon her fair young head,
And with the beasts she's sheltered, earth-forsaken
  And unesteemed, as the forgotten dead.
Yet not alone—one friend whom God had chosen,
  One faithful, fervent human heart is there;
One, the eternal Father's own vicegerent,
  Is there to guard her with most tender care.
She kneels in prayer, the damp, chill cave her shelter,
  While the wild wind drives in the cold night-rain,
Yet a new sense of bliss fills all her being,
  A new, deep joy that hallows want and pain.
She kneels in prayer—the one supremest hour
  Of all time's life of agonies and joys
Comes—the Redeemer comes, and God's dear mercy
  The power of evil in its might destroys.

Night never was so blessed—that lowly maiden
   With her pure soul so lifted to its Lord,
And all her being wrapt in adoration,
   Is she, the Mother of the Eternal Word!
Yes, her young life knows a new nameless rapture,
   A joy no other human heart hath known:
The Virgin is a Mother—the Eternal
   Clothed in her flesh is hers, her child, her own.
She sees Him, He is hers, hers only,
   The very life He lives is part of hers;
She sees Him, He is hers, her own, hers only,
   There is no joy like that her heart now stirs.
She sees Him! light hath come, it glows, it brightens,
   And angel-worshippers bend down in awe;
And heaven visits earth, earth's poorest homestead,
   Where God the Son lies cradled upon straw.
His tiny arms are raised to seek for shelter,
   Sweetly to find it in that bosom blest,
Where close in trembling bliss her love enfolds Him
   To find on earth His fittest place of rest.
His baby-lips speak love in wordless language,
   His eyes, so all-unutterably sweet,
Open in mercy—now the eyes of Jesus
   And those of Mary for the first time meet.
His feet, those rosy infant feet are warmed
   Within the pressure of His Mother's hand;
And to her heart she holds Him, while archangels
   Listen in awe to hear His first command.
But His heart listens for her voice—His Mother's,
   That voice more dear than heaven's chorus-songs,—
Her heart responds to His—she asks for mercy
   For all His creatures in their countless throngs.
Mercy for all, the sinless and the sinful,
   The wayward and the wild, the sad of heart,
The squanderers of life's best gifts, and mercy
   And peace for all who choose the better part.

By the dear hour when you first caressed Him,
    When first the Sacred Heart beat close to thine,
By His first-uttered word, thy name, sweet Mother,
    In bonds of His dear love our hearts entwine!
By the remembrance of His rosy fingers
    Playing among the tresses of thy hair,
And by His infant loveliness, oh hear us!
    Speak to His heart for us a mother's prayer!

TO A YOUNG RELIGIOUS.

A DAY of suffering is a day of blessings,
    If it but draw us to the Sacred Heart;
Gladly we cling to life's most dread distresses,
    If death may lead us from them far apart.

Even from your patron's feast, dear child of sorrow,
    In spite of all our prayers and all our love,
Suffering contrives a keener zest to borrow,
    Sooner to fit you for the realms above.

Methought the vows, the veil, the consecration,
    Had seen an end to sorrow and to pain,
But every pang seems the reiteration
    Of sorrow past but to begin again.

It must be well. —'Twas thus that Aloysius
    Self-sacrificed, accomplished all God's will,
And thus, my eldest child, *my* Aloysius;
    Doth mercy lead you with divinest skill.

KYRIE ELEISON.

" Kyrie eleison "—loneliness and sorrow
    Fill the old halls that we have loved so long,
" Kyrie eleison,"—earthly lights are fading,
    Lost 'mid the night clouds, darkling as they throng.

" Kyrie eleison"—oh, great God, have mercy,
    Have mercy on us, for no common woe
Shrouds us in agony and bows our spirits,
    And thrills our hearts with aching throe on throe.

Mercy, Lord Jesus—memory keeps recalling
    Faces beloved, hearts trusted not in vain;
Affection with its fairy hues keeps painting
    Scenes that have been, but may not be again.

And gratitude with tendrils never broken,
    Seeks vainly, vainly, for the long-loved bough,
Its life that was so cheering and so graceful,
    Is but a power to torture being now.

Mercy, O Lord, have mercy—let the anguish,
    The life-long weariness be mine, but bless
With all the fulness of Thy heart's best graces
    Her whom we love, in all her loneliness.

Bless her, dear Lord—let tenderest compassion
    O'erwhelm that strong, self-trusting, loving heart,
Oh rain on her Thy mercies, 'till she feels them,
    And owns how good, how merciful Thou art.

5

TO SAINT MADELEINE.

St. Madeleine, St. Madeleine,
  So blest through all the years,
Since over Jesus' feet you poured
  Those floods of heart-wrung tears!
Since first through that fair human face
  You saw the Godhead shine,
And heard in those sweet human words
  A voice that was divine.

A voice that called thee *to* His heart,
  That chose thee for His own.
A look that saw thy place within
  The halo of His throne.
Saint Madeleine, Saint Madeleine,
  Life's wild illusions die;
Earth-weary, unto Jesus' feet
  Methinks I see thee fly.

No word—oh not a single word,
  No word but flowing tears—
No word, for He is God, He sees
  The story of those years.
Over the blessed feet that trod
  The thorny path of pain,
Through all life's wilderness for us,
  It falls, that saving rain.

And soon the dark, far-falling hair
  In radiant silken folds
Hath wrapped the feet of God on earth,
  Of Him earth's doom who holds!
The perfume of Arabia streams
  Upon them as she kneels,
And now her lips have touched His feet,
  Her bleeding heart He heals.

Then silently, all silently,
    And tremblingly, yet still,
Transformed into a saint, she stands
    The creature of His will.
Saint Madeleine, Saint Madeleine,
    By that sweet hour of grace,
And by the mercy of His heart,
    The glory of His face,

And by the everlasting love
    He be..   thee and thine,
Plead for our sisters on this day,
    Their hearts in His enshrine.
Ask for them graces such as bring
    His creatures nearest Him,
Ask for them lights that make the light
    Of earthly science dim.

Let strength be given them from above
    To realize His will,
To do their own appointed work
    With more than human skill;
Pray that the dews of heaven descend
    Upon their home and heart,
And that God's gracious love may be
    To them "the better part."

LIZZIE'S DREAM.

FOUNDED ON FACT.

SHE dreamed she was a princess,
    A sovereign, a queen,
And that she sat in royal state
    Where kings of old had been;

Through gorgeous windows, purple light
   And sunny amber hues
A glory that seemed not of earth
   O'er all around diffuse.
On old armorial bearings
   It gleams, and flags that waved
Where England's boasted chivalry
   Her proudest foes had braved.
They're shaken now, but not in war,
   Sweet thrills of music stream
Like winds through all their foldings,
   As through the maiden's dream.
She dreamed she was a princess,
   That men of haughty brow
Bend lowly there before her
   With the fealty of a vow;
That Tudor and Plantagenet,
   Stanley and Talbot—all
The knightly names of England
   With her will stand or fall.
Around her stands a chosen band
   Of maidens, fair as spring,
The incense of affection
   The offering they bring—
And Lizzie's dream seems real,
   She reigns an empress now,
She feels the sceptre in her hand,
   The crown upon her brow.
Sudden that crowd of courtiers
   Seems moved by something strange,
Its mood to one more solemn
   Seems wondrously to change;
Down all that ample centre
   Of Windsor's regal hall
Noble and knight and lady
   Bow down as back they fall.

With firmest step and bearing,
  Some purpose calm and high
Fixing the meaning of his face,
  The light within his eye,
A priest of God advances,
  To all but her unknown,
Who reigns to-day with heart elate
  A queen upon her throne.
All hearts are hushed, for now he stands
  Alone before the queen—
He stands alone, a priest in might,
  A prophet in his mien.
And now he speaks—"O Lady,
  Sovereign of this fair land,
Behold this glass, how fleetly pass
  These grains of worthless sand!
Ah even so, the sands of life
  Are passing from your heart
To-day you die, aye, e'en to-day,
  Before its hours depart."
Like a white lily broken
  Before the thunder dread,
Meekly the monarch-maiden
  Bowed down her jewelled head;
And with a voice that faltered
  E'en as a maiden's might,
She only said, "My God, my God!
  What means this awful night?
There's darkness closing o'er me,
  O father, lone and dread
The path that lies so plainly
  Between me and the dead.
Oh, if that glorious faith were *true*,
  Which feigns that Jesus will
Hide all His hypostatic life
  Our failing hearts to fill;

That He Himself will turn to prayer
His creature's parting breath,
And that His life will live in ours
E'en while we drink in death—
Then, father, gladly could I cast
My royal robes away,
And lay this uncrowned head at rest
Among the meanest clay."
"My child, my fair, young. stricken flower,
That faith is nothing feigned,
'Tis truth itself, God's holy truth
Immortal and unstained;
Let me but pour the tide of life
In baptism o'er your soul,
'Twill drive those clouds of doubt as far
As arctic pole from pole;
Then while death plays his awful part
Around this baseless throne,
Jesus, the Bread of Life, its God,
Will claim you all His own."
She dreamed that she was dying,
And that the God of might,
Veiled in His sacramental guise,
Filled all her soul with light;
That Jesus was within her,
Her love, her hope, her stay,
His "Real Presence," light and strength
To guide her on her way.

NOTE.—A young girl who had been brought up a Protestant, was really led
to believe in the Blessed Sacrament by a dream like the above in substance.
Rev. Father Preston was the priest of whose appearance in the crowd she
dreamed, and he it was who afterwards baptized her.

"PULCHRA ES."

THOU art fair, O Virgin Mother,
    Virgin daughter of the Lord!
Spouse of the most Holy Spirit!
    Mother of the Eternal Word!

Thou art fair—He hath adorned thee
    As His chosen resting-place;
He hath crowned thee, He hath blessed thee,
    As the glory of thy race.

Thou art fair, O Virgin Mother!
    With the beauty nature knows,
With the blushing of its blossoms,
    With the whiteness of its snows; *

With its inward hidden treasures,
    With its mystic mines of thought,
With its manifold affections
    To our wondrous union wrought.

Thou art fair, O Virgin Mother!
    Fair, for innocence is thine,
And God's own divinest Spirit
    Made thine infant heart His shrine.

"Pulchra es"—oh, thou art fairest,
    For within thee Jesus dwelt,
While around thee hosts of angels
    In adoring silence knelt.

Thou art fair, for He hath loved thee
    With a love He gives to none
But to thee, as thy Creator,
    And thy Saviour and thy Son!

---

* "My beloved is white and ruddy."

He was thine! within thy bosom
　　He hath rested, He hath lain,
Filling with divine effulgence
　　All thy being, heart and brain.

The green earth was blooming round thee
　　With its shining seas and streams,
With its music-shaken forests
　　Drinking in the bright sunbeams—

What were these to thee, sweet Mother?
　　For thy Jesus was thine own,
Thou wert His and He was reigning,
　　In thy heart as on His throne.

Thou art fair, O Virgin Mother!
　　Fairer in those mystic years,
When thy love grew strong and stronger,
　　'Neath the rain of blood and tears.

Fair, when crucified in spirit,
　　Thou wert standing by His cross,
While around His own mad creatures
　　Their insulting banners toss.

Fair, when rapt in adoration
　　And in anguish deep and dread,
Thou hast offered Him a ransom
　　For the living and the dead.

On thy pale hands fell the blood drops,
　　On thy vesture, on thy veil;
And the mother's heart is broken,
　　Yet is heard no woman's wail.

O sweet Mother, dearest Mother,
　　Sweetest fruit of Jesus' heart!
Stem the floods that sweep our spirit,
　　Thou—how powerful thou art!

We too, dearest, tenderest Mother,
　We must love thy Jesus too,
We must stand, and standing suffer
　With unquailing hearts, like you.

Pray, mother, that our spirits,
　May be strong and stand erect,
While life's loveliest affections,
　One by one, are wrung and wrecked.

"Lord, Thou knowest that we love Thee,"
　That we give Thee heart and soul,
Mind and will, and strength and spirit,
　Thine to master and control.

Make us love Thee, make us love Thee,
　Make our hearts become a flame,
That will burn into our being
　All the sweetness of Thy name.

Make us love Thee, like Augustine,
　When that great and gifted heart
Loved the most and sprung to meet Thee,
　And to know Thee as Thou art.

TO A LADY ON THE DEATH OF HER BETROTHED.

Not as I will, but as Thou wilt,
　Not as nature's heart would fain,
But as God's dear will ordaineth:
　Thus our loss will be as gain.

5*

Not as life-long love desireth;
  For affection true and tried,
Bound in bonds for Thee, Lord Jesus,
  At Thy feet must still abide;

To Thy heart must trace its well-spring,
  In Thy bosom find its rest,
In Thy heaven its consummation,
  In Thy presence first be blessed.

Lord, Thy will be done; if early,
  Sadly, thus we're doomed to part,
Let us meet near Thee in heaven,
  There to love Thee heart to heart.

There to bless Thee for the mercy
  Every sorrow meant, each pain;
There to see why Thou wouldst sever
  All the ties that yet remain.

Sister-love, all pure and stainless,
  Thou wouldst have me sunder too—
She is gone who would have stayed me,
  Lord, with tender thoughts of You.

Yet the kindly ocean bears me
  Oft the perfume of her heart;
New, unknown, yet loving sisters
  In her love for me have part.

Then Thy will be done, my Jesus,
  In Thy home but let us meet,
James and Mary and Helena,
  In Thy bosom, at Thy feet.

APPEAL TO A MOTHER.

MOTHER, do the Christmas carols
   Bring back Christmas days gone by ?
Happy days, my own loved mother—
   Oh, how quickly did they fly !

Sweet and low a silvery cadence
   Whispered to my girlish heart,
And I felt, my own loved mother,
   That our paths must be apart.

Christmas days brought thoughts of Jesus,
   Jesus as a helpless child ;
From the joys of home's dear fireside
   Then I longed to be exiled.

Christmas night I saw the stable
   And the poor and lowly bed ;
Mother darling, then your daughter
   Vowed to veil this proud young head.

Vowed to leave life's dearest treasures,
   For He had left all for me—
Vowed to live a life of labor,
   Burst my fetters and be free.

Free from earth's soft silken fetters,
   Leaving love itself for love,
Looking forward, mother darling,
   To a loving home above.

Mother, my own mother, inly
   Bled your child's too-loving heart,
Bled to leave thee, bled to lose thee,
   Loved and honored as thou art.

Scenes of childhood's halcyon hours
   Memory painted o'er and o'er,
Mother darling, you and Minna,
   Dearer than in days of yore.

Naples and its leafy vineyards,
   Fancy traversed by your side,
Sat with you, my own loved mother,
   By the sun-bespangled tide.

Listened to the sea's sad music,
   Heard your voice so soft and sweet,
Garlanded your hair with flowers,
   Played a fairy at your feet.

Grew a girl and grew a woman,
   Saw through life's thin, silvery veil,
Lower-toned than its rejoicings,
   Heard the spirit's yearning wail.

Then the voice of Jesus called me,
   Called me to be His alone,
Called me to His mystic nuptials,
   Chose me to be near His throne.

Ah, sweet mother, oft your daughter
   Told you of that thrilling call,
Told you she must answer bravely,
   Must relinquish earth's poor all.

Must be His who deigned to choose her,
   Must, like Him, be crucified,
Must retrace the *Via Crucis*,
   Reach the mount on which He died.

Mother, now another Christmas
. Finds me resting at His feet,
Wanting but my mother's blessing,
To make all my bliss complete.

Ah! dear mother, by the memory
Of your Christmas blessings past,
Come and bless your little Cecy,
Bless and heal her heart at last.

And may heaven's choicest blessings,
God's divinest holiest grace,
Dower all your days in mercy,
Till you meet Him face to face.

TO A FRIEND.

By the sorrows we have known,
By the memories round us thrown,
By the cruel, crushing loss
That has been our killing cross:
Sister, fellow-sufferer, friend,
May our future sorrows blend.

May we strive together well,
Bound by the same sacred spell,
The same sacred veil and vows,
The same divine immortal Spouse:
Sister, fellow-sufferer, friend,
Thus our hearts together blend.

Blend in purpose and in love,
Blend in looking earth above,
Blend in fear and blend in hope,
Blend with evil still to cope:
Sister, fellow-sufferer, share
Still the cross that I must bear.

Are those blended lives to part,
Living each with lonely heart?
Is it God's most holy will
All our heart-hopes thus to kill?
Yes, "to suffer or to die"
Is the true soul's thirsting cry.

To do, to suffer all God's will,
Led by love's divinest skill;
Suffer bravely, suffer lone,
Life and sorrow soon are gone;
Soon this aching life shall cease
And our hearts shall find release.

Thus St. Gertrude lived and died,
Bound to Jesus crucified;
Thus Augustine's burning heart
Burst the ties of life apart:
Sister, fellow-sufferer, friend,
In God's love our lives shall blend.

ST. GERTRUDE'S FEAST.

St. Gertrude's Feast again, but not the graces,
  The affluence of love that was her own!
Rather sad memories of times and places
  Still clasp the realms of thought as with a zone,—

A frigid zone, without the borealis
  And the strange splendors of the northern night,
The gleaming starlight and the ice-built palace—
  All nature dead and cold, yet clear and bright.

Our life, too, centres towards a pole supernal,
  That Sacred Heart, which dear St. Gertrude made
The pole of her existence—love eternal,
  Before whose splendors all earth's glories fade.
That Heart alone is true—time, grief, misfortune,
  Effect no change in that unchanging heart:
Dear sister, may our years and cares and sorrows
  Make us as true, together or apart.

THE VERY FLOWERS ARE STRANGERS.

"The very stars are strangers."—MISS LANDON.

THE very flowers are strangers; though so lovely,
  They are not those my childhood knew so well;
Not the white snowdrop, tremulous and pearly,
  The wild wood-hyacinth, the frail bluebell—
They are not here, the field-flowers I have gathered,
  Namelessly beautiful of scent and hue,
The heather-bells that purple the proud mountains,
  The dear hedge-roses with their gems of dew.

Here is no woodbine, no wild honeysuckle,
  That gathers round the old and hoary trees,
Wraps their stern trunks in wreaths of graceful blossom,
  Wins them the worship of the birds and bees;
No dear laburnum blossoms, golden, pensile,
  With their soft weight bending the green, slight stems,
No hawthorn boughs, as fragrant as Mount Carmel's
  No daisies strewn around like scattered gems.

Not the green grass itself—a world of beauty
   Untreasured and unthought of does it hide;
Blossoms minutely lovely, well I knew them
   Ere the wild sea of life reached its full tide.
The mystic shamrock leaves grow greenly through it,
   And crimson clover, fragrant, honey-sweet,
And the white mushrooms, white as snow first fallen—
   The fairy queen might choose them for her seat.

And so they say she does, for they are growing
   Whitest in places consecrate to her,
Places no peasant foot would dare to tread on,
   For fairy ire is something dread to stir.
Alas, the wide, free fields, the young oats silvery
   And green and shining in the clear June light,
And the blue bending flax-flowers and the meadows
   Jewelled with blossoms beautiful and bright.

The sunny rills! I see them; they are flowing
   On to the bosom of that deep blue lake,
They long to lave the marble water-lilies,
   The quiet of their placid lives to break.
Cold, calm, white water-lilies—look within them,
   Deep in that chalice lies the type of love;
So in pure hearts there lives the love of Jesus,
   A love that lifts them all earth-life above.

Alas, my own green Erin!—a few flowers,
   A few green tendrils drew thy daughter home,
Home to thy heart again, my own green Erin,
   Cinctured by the wild ocean's snowy foam.
What is this old word *home?* what is this clinging
   To things that pass away and perish soon?
Is it ourselves we love, our life's sweet morning,
   And all the sunshine of its flowery noon?

Oh is it I, my own young life, I'm loving,
  Thus in remembering my native land,
Gathering the golden blossoms of affection
  That made life's margin like a silvery strand ?
Yet onward lay the ocean, stormy, cloud-clad,
  Surging and sweeping, bearing many a freight,
And hiding broken hearts within its bosom—
  Sharing the awfulness of many a fate.

Oh may that sweeping ocean bear me onward,
  Onward to thee, the beautiful, the true;
May its salt waters blot out all resistance
  To Thy sweet will, and let me live to you!
Let me, oh let me spend myself to buy thee
  The hearts thou prizest, oh so dearly well;
The little children—let me live to save them,
  Flowers for the gardens where thy loved ones dwell.

Fresh field-flowers, pure and stainless, ah, my Jesus,
  Will You not let us gather them for Thee ?
Will You not aid us, bless us, give us courage ?
  Say but the word, and they Thine own shall be.
Say but the word, and worldly hearts shall soften
  Into sweet pity for the children's woes,
And learn to aid us in this loving effort
  To make the desert blossom as the rose.

ON READING REV. DR. ANDERDON'S TRANSLA-
TION OF THE BISHOP OF ORLEANS' SERMON
ON THE EVICTIONS IN IRELAND.

Text—"Ite, angeli veloces, ad gentem convulsam et dilaceratam . . . ad
gentem expectantem et conculcatam."
"Go, ye swift angels, to a nation rent and torn in pieces . . . to a nation
expecting and trodden under foot."—*Isaias*, xviii, 2.

Go, ye swift angels, angels of God's mercy,
  Laden with love and tenderness and grace,
Go to our stricken land, our ruined people,
  Go to our wronged and desolated race.

Ite—oh go, go to my native Erin,
  Go to wild Erris, where the golden gorse
And purple heather bloom, as if destruction
  Filled not the land with sorrow and remorse.

Oh, blessed angels, go—they know no healing
  But that you bear upon your golden wings;
Go, ere the demon of oppression darken
  The whole green isle with the fell cloud he flings.

Go to where Connamara hides her sorrow
  Within the shadow of historic hills,
The sea's wild voice blending with cries of anguish
  Borne down on all her silver-shining rills.

Borne from the ruined homes along the borders,
  Borne from the breaking hearts that say farewell
To home and hope, and all but faith's aspirings,
  And go in far off lands alone to dwell.

Blessed are ye, swift angels, ye can reach her,
  The martyr of the nations, where she stands,
Smiles blending with her tears, sublimely faithful,
  True in each sacrifice that God demands.

Yes, you can bring the precious blood of Jesus,
   His merits and His grace to still her woes,
From His pierced heart its priceless love to win her,
   To keep her strong until her conflict close.

Jam hiems transiit—would that through her homesteads
   These blessed words might sound from shore to shore,
That bigotry and hate might be extinguished,
   And faith and peace reign all the island o'er.

Ite—swift Angels, go, oh go to Erin,
   Tell her our prayers ascend to heaven with hers,
That in our hearts her faith, her love is living,
   And that her woe our heart-affections stirs.

Oh to my own, my beautiful, my darling,
   My lost, my long-beloved native land,
Bear her child's love, her prayers, and all her labors,
   While life ebbs out on this far foreign strand.

THE TRANSFIGURATION.

" And they, lifting up their eyes, saw no one but only Jesus."
                                ST. MATT., xvii, 8.

No one but Jesus, but our blest Redeemer,
   No one but Jesus, our most blessed Lord!
No one but Jesus Christ, the Son of justice,
   Jesus the Son of God, the Christ, the Word.
Oh what was earth to them and all its beauties,
   The creatures of His hand and of His will,
For they saw Jesus in the light of heaven,
   There on that beauteous Galilean hill ?
" They, lifting up their eyes, saw only Jesus,"
   His face divine, so human and so fair,
They saw those eyes so lit with love and mercy,
   Saw heaven's own sunbeams gild His radiant hair.

They saw Him on Mount Thabor in His glory,
  White wondrous angels bent from heaven in awe,
While James and John and Peter, looking upward,
  Knew 'twas their Saviour and their God they saw.
Knew Him, thus all transfigured, and adored Him,
  While Peter cried from his ecstatic heart,
Oh let us be here always, for 'tis heaven,
  'Tis heaven, Lord Jesus, whereso'er Thou art.
They saw Thee, Jesus, and they heard Thee speaking
  Of Calvary, of suffering and of shame,
While Moses and Elias bent adoring,
  As near Thee in the radiant cloud they came.
Oh, shall we see Thee in the bliss of heaven,
  Shall we, Thy consecrated children, kneel
On heaven's golden floor to kiss Thy footprints,
  And heaven's dear joy in these poor bosoms feel ?

TO SISTER MARY BERNARD R——, A LITTLE BEFORE HER DEATH.

The narrow path! it winds through sorrows many,
  'Tis bordered close by precipices dark ;
Yet tread it fearless, at its glorious summit
  The Heart of Jesus is the home, the ark.

From the wild steep of Ararat descending,
  The saved ones entered on a life of care ;
But the saved soul shall never know returning—
  The sacred Heart, her resting place is there.

For you the way is short, however rugged,
  A few short months, and trial shall be o'er ;
My novice child, my dear, young, suffering sister,
  Soon shall sweet peace be yours for evermore.

Soon shall the cross that wounds these poor young
    shoulders,
  Be laid rejoicingly at Jesus' feet,
And this dear aching head, so soon earth-weary,
  Shall wear a crown, for virgins only meet.

Courage, dear child, thus blessedly selected
  From our dear consecrated novice-band;
Jesus Himself is calling—go to meet Him:
  Farewell! thy home is in "the better land."

There pray for me, my sister, pray to Jesus,
  That soon, oh soon, my place may be with you,
Away from sin and sorrow and temptation,
  At rest with Him whose love alone is true.

TO AN UNFAITHFUL MEMBER OF THE SACRED HEART CONFRATERNITY.

O Sacred Heart of Jesus! Heart forsaken
  On your own day, by one You dearly prize,
By one who promised to be ever faithful,
  Whose heart was crimsoned with Thy blood's rich dyes.

O Sacred Heart! no hour of adoration
  Was passed before Thee by Thy child this day;
No mass, no sweet communion was her portion—
  Hear me, oh hear, while, agonized, I pray.

I pray, O Sacred Heart! that soon the spirit
  Of sacrifice may come to this dear soul,
That she may learn to take her cross and follow
  Thy steps until she reach the heavenly goal.

SUFFERING.

SILENTLY to suffer,
  Cheerfully to bear
Hidden, heart-felt sorrow:
  This is virtue rare.

Only love of Jesus,
  Only His sweet grace,
To such high endeavor
  Can the spirit brace.

But when such He sends us,
  Special aid He sends,
Such as He but offers
  To His chosen friends.

Strange, heart-breaking sorrows,
  Such as few have known,
Are for souls called nearest
  To His awful throne.

Suffer then, my darling,
  And rejoice to bring
Thus your heart the closer
  To your Lord and King.

Count it joy to suffer
  All God's holy will,
Say, with Job, "I trust Thee,
  Even if Thou kill."

THE CONVERSION OF ST. PAUL.

A scion of old Judea,
  A child of the chosen race,
He honored the ancient fathers,
  He honored their dwelling place;
He loved the majestic temple
  Where Israel worshipped God,
The incense that veiled its altars,
  The flowers of Aaron's rod;

The song of Miriam thrilled him,
  And Jeremiah's woe
Had softened oft his spirit,
  In boyhood long ago;
He longed for the promised Ruler,
  He panted to see him lead
The people to wealth and glory,
  To see them from thraldom freed—

Freed from the Roman's fetters,
  Solomon's reign restored,
Power and peace and plenty
  Over the land outpoured;
Yet turned him in proud defiance
  Away from the light that shone,
Scorning the meek Redeemer,
  The faith that His blood hath sown.

Out in the Syrian splendor,
  Filled with his fiery zeal,
Rode he with warriors round him,
  Banners and flashing steel.
" Down with these hated Christians,
  Let *them* like their leader die,"—
This was his beacon onward,
  This was his wild war-cry.

Hushed in the lap of summer,
  Mountain and valley lay,
The bright-hued birds were hiding
  From the noon of the torrid day;
All but that wild heart rested,
  All but its owner smiled;
'Mong the green leaves the zephyr
  Breath'd like a sleeping child.

Hark! there's a voice from heaven,
  'Tis not a trumpet tone;
See! there's a flood of radiance
  Full on that proud head thrown;
Stricken he bows, he flings him
  Down on the burning sod,
The voice is the voice of Jesus,
  The light is the light of God.

Then in that light supernal,
  Truth at its source he saw,
The madness of earthly wisdom,
  The light of the new-born law;
He flings from his heart the passions,
  That bore him so fiercely on,
The darkness they wrapped around him
  For ever is past and gone.

Gladly he casts the glory,
  The love of the world aside,
To know but the love of Jesus,
  And Jesus crucified;
Apostle of Jew and Gentile,
  He brings unto crowds and kings
The law and the love of Jesus,
  The peace in their path that springs.

Oh! for the glorious spirit
  That gave as a holocaust
The being that God had given,
  So long to His service lost:
That never looked back, and kept not
  Of earth and its stains a taint,
But lost in Thy love, Redeemer,
  Became in its light a saint.

Oh! for his glorious spirit,
  To gather like him to Thee.
With patience, and love, and labor,
  The *lambs* from Thy fold that flee;
To lift them up in our arms,
  And lay them before Thy throne,
To comfort, and heal, and save them,
  And make them at last Thine own.

NIGHT THOUGHTS.

HAVE you ever gazed at midnight
  On a dark yet glorious sky,
Where within the cloud-made valleys
  The stars in myriads lie?

Have you gazed till they grew nearer,
  And clearer, and more bright,
And you saw strange constellations
  With wonder and delight?

Have you gazed in early summer
  On a meadow in the sun,
While the soft wind made its masses
  Like billows seem to run?

6

Have you seen the hidden flowers
  Gleam brightly here and there,
Until gold and purple blossoms
  Gemmed its surface everywhere—

And the song-birds soared above it,
  And the zephyrs chorused round,
And the perfume of the summer
  Seemed mingled with the sound ?

Have you seen the green assuming
  A thousand varied shades,
As the sunbeams through the openings
  Pierced the forest's dim arcades ?

Gazing upward long and longer,
  You begin to see the birds
Whose clear carol through the branches
  Sooth'd your heart like kindly words.

Oh, 'tis thus that gazing upward
  On the spiritual world,
By degrees the veils that hide it
  From our vision are unfurled.

By degrees its hidden glories
  Break upon our mortal eyes,
And we see the stars that glisten
  In heaven's mysterious skies.

SAINT FRANCIS OF ASSISIUM.

SAINT FRANCIS, favorite of the Infant Jesus,
  Weeping in Bethlehem hot tears that tell
How deep the springs of love and self-devotion,
  In that seraphic heart, that throb and swell.

Saint Francis, lover of the poor and simple,
    Friend of the birds, the lambs, the turtle-doves;
Brother of all God's works, so fond and tender,
    So full of sweet and holy, fervent loves.

Loves that were all for Jesus, Jesus only,
    Loves that made earth a holy, sacred place,
A temple to God's glory, full of worship,
    Open to every tribe and every race.

Saint Francis, wed to poverty, for Jesus
    Was poor on earth, and thou wouldst be like Him;
And then He came to thee and brought thee heaven,
    And made all this poor world look cold and dim.

Saint Francis, crucified with love for Jesus,
    With hands and feet all wounded like your Lord's,
St. Francis, drawing thousands to His service
    By the sweet power of your ways and words.

Dearest Saint Francis!—home-love makes me love thee,
    For she, my sainted sister, bore thy name,
And loved her God and all His simple creatures
    With a sweet love *like* thine, if not the same.

And *now* her child and *mine* delights to bear it,
    And loves to follow in the path she trod;
Bound by the same dear vows to the same service,
    The service of her Saviour and her God.

Bless her, Saint Francis, make her ever faithful,
    Zealous and earnest till this life is o'er,
And at the feet of Jesus and of Mary
    She kneels a bride, on heaven's golden floor.

OLD TIMES.

THE world seemed clad with flowers
  And light when I was young,
And all the happy hours,
   Each hailed a hope new-sprung.

Joyous and smiling sweetly
  The future beckoned on;
While our young footsteps fleetly
  Bounded its paths along.

And often we used to cluster,
  The grass our fragrant seat,
Screened from the sun's hot lustre,
  To tell of some fairy feat.

To vow that no time should part us,
  To laugh at all thought of care,
Oh! 'twas sad in our bliss to start us
  With the presence of sorrow there.

Those vows are broken, for parted
  By fate, by sea, and stream,
Are the friends so sanguine-hearted,
  That met in that early dream.

Oh, sad is the change come o'er us,
  For that old familiar place
Rings no more with our merry chorus—
  'Tis the home of a stranger race.

They have trodden down all our flowers,
  Hewn down our favorite tree,
And the place of our pleasant bowers
  'Twere a sorrow now to see.

Shall such sorrow be repeated
  In our short, fleeting life,
Of its dearest hopes still cheated
  When they were most warm and rife.

No more does my fancy's dreaming
  Bright cloudless visions bring,
They are scattered and crushed, yet gleaming
  Like pearls off their broken string.

ASPIRATION.

WHEN shall this soul which Thou hast wed,
For which Thou'st labored, lived, and bled,
Be purified, be worthy Thee,
From all its fatal earth-stains free ?

When shall it seek no heart but Thine,
With Thy sweet will its will entwine ?
When suffer for Thy sake in peace,
When burst its bonds and find release ?

Dear Lord, what am I ? veil and vows
Mark out Thy creature as Thy spouse!
Thy chosen one, Thine own! allied
And bound to Thee the Crucified.

O God of mercy, God of might,
My spirit trembles at its height;
Lord Jesus, I had been in hell,
Hadst Thou not loved me all too well.

Hadst Thou not caught me up and saved
The soul o'er which earth's banners waved,
And gathered up this shattered heart,
And healed it with Thy mercy's art.

And made me love Thee, made me know
The evil and the bitter woe
Of having wandered far from Thee,
And sought in bondage to be free.

At last, oh make me all Thine own,
Burst every tie but this alone;
All I have loved are sundered far—
Be Thou my waning life's sole star.

A DREAM.

I SEE a queenly form
    Through my dreams,
Around her sorrow's storm
    Wildly streams;
That look once calm and loving,
That scarce could seem reproving
Without my whole heart moving,
    Coldly gleams.

A gentle voice is speaking.
    Lo! I hear,
Thy voice, my own loved mother,
    Low and clear;
Strange, awful words are spoken,
The heart so early broken,
From its short peace awoken,
    Chills with fear.

A long-loved name is mingling
    With each thought,
Thy blessed name, sweet mother,
    Sorrow-fraught;

I breathe it not, thou'rt dead,
Thy spirit far hath fled.
Those cold tears, cold as lead,
   Come unsought.

That form is bending sadly
   O'er my bed.
That hand is laid in blessing
   On my head;
That heart bemoans this grief,
Which cannot know relief,
Till life's hours sad and brief
   All have sped.

I wake, no queenly form
   Bendeth near,
I list, no mother's voice
   So blest I hear;
O God of mercy, guide
The heart thus crucified,
While o'er life's surging tide
   Death draweth near!

ON RECEIVING SOME SHAMROCK LEAVES FROM HOME.

O WILLVILLE! Willville! into this dim exile,
 So long and lone, thy dear green leaves have come,
Thy sweet green shamrock leaves, as if to win me
 Back to the thought of Erin and of home.

Back to thy long-loved lake, thy dear hills folded
 In such a wealth of soft, luxuriant green,
And the bright water musical, and silvery,
 Flashing like lines of light those hills between.

The wild "Red Bracs," "Romany" and "Rockeira,"
And all the loving, faithful people there,
Come to my thought; and then the quiet churchyard,
The graves—the dead—my father resting there.

Dear Killivane, so quaint and true and loving
Thy people's ways and words seem now to me,
That the strange city grows more strange than ever,
And the old places dearer seem to be.

Willville, our beautiful, our loved, lost Willville!
Twenty-three years of exile cannot tear
From out thy child's lone heart that fairy picture,
Nor the sweet memories that are nestling there.

God bless the dear old land, the dear old people,
God bless their hearts and homes each day anew,
God keep them in their faith and in their country,
And keep them unto *both* for ever true!

TO THE BLESSED VIRGIN!

O MARY, by thy life divine,
Thy beatific grace,
And by the light of Jesus' eyes,
The beauty of His face;
Oh by its likeness unto thine,
Its nearness unto thee,
And by thy joy, His shrine on earth,
His chosen shrine to be.

Sweet Mother Mary! win the souls
He lived for, to His love,
And lift their hopes this passing world
And all its joys above.

Bring to His love the innocent,
The young, the pure of heart,
O sweetest Mary, save them,
By thy mother-love's sweet art!

Bring to His worship loving hearts,
Self-sacrificing, true,
Life-saddened, with eternity
And God alone in view.
Teach them, through all the realms of thought,
To seek for garlands rare,
That they may consecrate to Him
Life's lovely things and fair.

The lovely things that fancy finds
In fairy regions strange,
When far from this dull, work-day world
She ventures free to range.
Pictures of Bethlehem she'll find,
Of Joseph and of thee,
And of thy strange Egyptian home,
Far o'er th' historic sea.

Of Nazareth—of Thabor,
Of Calvary—the Cross,
The death, the grave, the Magdalen,
Wild with the pain of loss—
The loss of His sweet presence
Who saved her and who blest
Her broken spirit with His peace,
Her broken heart with rest.

Treasures like these—oh teach us,
To gather and to gild
With love's adorning, till our hearts
With God's dear love are filled.
6*

Farewell, sweet Mother, 'tis the last,
The last, last song my heart
May sing on earth—my poet-life
Hath lost its long-loved art.

CHRISTMAS THOUGHTS.

I SOMETIMES gaze on the crib and stall
Where lies the Lord and Master of all
As a helpless babe, while His right hand holds
The ruins of so many countless worlds;
But soon I turn to the dark hill-side
Where hangs my Jesus crucified.

I mark, in awe, His helpless form
Who rules the tempest and guides the storm;
Now the mighty warrior is taking His rest,
As a peaceful lamb on his mother's breast:
But yet I fly to the dark hill-side,
Where hangs my Jesus crucified.

I kiss the tiny feet with humble love,
They tread the vaulted heavens above,
Whilst here poor swathing bands confine
Them closely bound to Mercy's shrine;
But even now I turn aside
To embrace the feet of the Crucified.

I look at the downy head and sigh,
It is crowned with unnumbered stars on high,
Whilst it lies below on a throbbing heart
Which already feels the incipient dart;
With a guilty pang I turn aside
To the cross of the bleeding Crucified.

To the gentle heart I prostrate bow,
'Tis a burning furnace in heaven now;
The centre of the Trinity divine
Here doth an Infant's form enshrine;
In speechless wonder I turn aside
And fly to the feet of the Crucified.

We may gaze life-long on a scene so fair,
But it is not I must linger there;
'Tis a scene where light and joy have part,
Delighting the innocent and pure of heart:
True penitent love must ever abide,
At the feet of Jesus crucified.

M. C. S.

THE THREE "HAIL MARYS."

'Tis past the vesper hour, now the starry, solemn night
Comes with sweet, resistless power, and with clear and
    paly light,
Which the weary world of labor a boon thrice blessed
    deems,
While neighbor wishes neighbor "good night and
    pleasant dreams;"
And household bands are kneeling to bless the Lord of
    might
For the day which He is sealing with the sable hand of
    night.
Oh it 'minds me of an hour, an hour of solemn prayer,
When not a single flower decked the Mohawk's valley
    fair,
When the giant hills had muffled their topmost peaks in
    snow,
And the river all unruffled flowed on, the ice below,

Save where at Cohoes leaping and dashing in its play,
And myriad crystals heaping, it bounded on its way.
Of *Sisters* to each other who clung through weal and woe;
Of vain attempts to smother their grief that *one* must
        go,
The youngest, fairest flower of the old household tree,
Like to a summer shower, their tears fall fast and free.
Yet sought they not to keep her who to her Saviour's feet
With the one thankful leper had chosen to retreat.
But on that quiet even, though nature would have way,
They raised their hearts to heaven whose pleasures ne'er
        decay,
Beseeching of that Father who placed them exiles here,
That He again would gather, beyond the reach of fear,
That band so strewed, so scattered upon the face of
        earth,
Their pleasant home so shattered, so hushed its ancient
        mirth,
That He would reunite them where death shall be no
        more,
Where sorrow cannot blight them, where separation's
        o'er;
That near their gentle mother and by their father's side,
With their long-parted brothers they may for aye abide,
Together hymn His praises, together see His face,
Who sinful man upraises to fill the angels' place.
And while thus lowly kneeling in trustful prayer, they
        turned
To mercy's Queen appealing in those sweet accents
        learned
Of Gabriel, entreating that she for them would gain
That blessed and endless meeting, who never asks in vain.
And as a filial token, promised that wheresoe'er
The daily prayers were spoken through every coming
        year,

The *Aves* thrice repeated the same boon should implore,
And show how deeply seated the love that each one bore
To her most holy mother, whose tender heart so well
Knew beyond every other the bitter word, "farewell."
And then o'er earth and ocean the watchword passes on,
Thrilling with deep emotion those unto whom 'tis gone—
And she who thus is breaking the ties so fondly wound
By love beyond all speaking their sister hearts around—
Though she has sought with Mary to choose the "better part,"
Doth not her purpose vary, now that she must depart?
No, but her heart is saddened upon that parting eve
Afar from all that gladdened their childhood's home to leave
By that far foreign river, and 'mid those alien snows
Where, from the laden quiver of faith and country's foes,
A bitter dart has swept them, the sisters of her love.
Marvel not then she wept them, nor blame her, nor reprove,
For did she leave them wearing the birthright of her race?
Were they at home still sharing their own and rightful place,
Were their young brothers near them to shelter and defend,
And in her place to cheer them, their sister, playmate, friend?
'Twere not in tears she'd hail it the hour so long besought,
Nor would e'en nature quail at the now so trying thought
Of a long and lasting farewell to those on earth most dear:
Nor loved she the less truly, for shedding sorrow's tear,

The choice which she had taken, for it hath poured a
    light
O'er her young life unshaken, and steady, strong, and
    bright.
Years since that night have faded, but still the *Aves* are
Offered in green woods shaded, 'neath the lone evening
    star,
By a loved brother kneeling in the far, glowing West,
Many and old home-feelings waking within his breast.
In their own isle, the holy home of the martyr race,
Where God, who lifts the lowly, hath so long showered
    His grace;
Where the old Devenish tower in the blue lake of isles,
Like the undying flower, looks upon time and smiles;
Where Inniskeen's grey ruins and Lisgool's holy shade
Picture the spoilers' doings, where brave MacGuire swayed.
Soothing Christ's suffering members, breaking the Bread
    of Life,
One there is who remembers those whom the world's sad
    strife
Hath so far dashed asunder; and though in reverence he
The chastening rod bows under, still in the *Aves* three
Prayeth that in that dwelling where many mansions are,
And in the joy excelling our poor conceptions far,
He may in gladness meet them, and upon each one's
    brow
See, when he there shall greet them, crowns for their
    sorrows now.

SPRING.

A CREATURE of light and joy am I,
    Bringing life and freshness to earth and sky,
Like a fair sprite passing from land to land,
    Bestowing rich blessings with ready hand;

The mighty river that icebound lay
I bid leap out to the face of day,
And onward roll to the deep blue sea,
'Mid its bright waves making sweet melody.

To the mazy forests all grey and hoar
Their beautiful foliage I next restore,
And bring back the birds with their plumage gay
To swell with their soft notes sweet nature's lay.
Then I bid the flowers their petals ope
And shed perfume sweet as the balm of hope,
When first in the Christian soul it wakes,
And the beauty of God for its portion takes.

I am known to you all as the changeful Spring
A timid, half-smiling, half-tearful thing;
But mystery's mantle is o'er me thrown
And to few, alas! is its meaning known.
For I was there in olden time
When Gabriel came with the news sublime,
That the Word had come down from His royal throne
To make the frail nature of man His own.

And scarce had He opened His infant eyes,
More purely fair than Italian skies,
When I saw Him borne over desert sands,
To save Him from death at His creature's hands;
Again did I see Him when years had flown,
And the little babe to a man had grown,
Made the victim of those that He came to save
At the pillar, the cross, in the stranger's grave.

I beheld the thorns on His brow divine,
Saw the scourge with His sacred hair entwine,
Heard the sound of each cruel blow that drove
The nails through the hands of that God of love;

Heard His own sweet voice from the cross implore
Mercy for those who had shed His gore;
And mine was the sun that withheld its light
To mourn for the death of the Infinite.

I saw Him rise upon Easter morn
From among the dead, as the eldest born,
Robed in the glory, His own of yore,
But shrouded and hidden from man before;
His ascent from the mount it was mine to see,
And to hear, with the men of old Galilee,
"Let not your spirits be filled with woe,
He shall come again as you've seen Him go."

Then learn of the Spring, as it comes each year,
To have ever within you a holy fear,
And o'er Jesus' sorrows in love to weep,
Yet the joy of His grace in your hearts to keep;
That the crown of life He may grant to you
When He shall come making all things new,
As is faintly shadowed in happy Spring
When she breathes new life into every thing.

"SOUVENIR DE MISSION."

REMEMBER the Mission, my child, for thou
New fealty then to thy God did'st vow;
Squander not lightly the grace bestowed
When thy tears at the feet of thy Savior flowed.
If many the sins unto thee forgiven,
Heavy the chains from thy spirit riven,
If the debt remitted to thee was great,
Now let thy love be proportionate.

Remember "the mission cross" that stood
Wearing no longer the tinge of blood,
Lest thou in terror shouldst turn aside
Despairing, like Judas, the deicide;
But to dispel all thy vain alarms,
With the banner of peace on thy outstretched arms,
Promising mercy, and love, and grace
To those who themselves 'neath its shadow place.

Remember the thrilling words that fell,
Sounding the depths of thy soul so well,
From the envoys of peace from thy Father who
Sent forth His servants in search of you.
How bitter and evil it was for thee
Far from thy Father's love to flee,
To have offered that pearl beyond all price,
Thy soul, to Satan a sacrifice.

Remember the voice in the early morn
Teaching thee how to extract the thorn,
That stung thy conscience with bitter pain,
Goading it on to yet deeper stain;
Showing the way to be bright and clear
Which had appeared to thee dark and drear,
Bidding thee cheerfully bear the cross,
Counting all other gain as loss.

Remember the upraised crucifix
Though thou daredst not on it thy gaze to fix,
But with Duke William of Aquitaine,*
Fell at the feet of thy Lord again.

* In allusion to the celebrated conversion of the Duke of Aquitaine, by St.
Bernard.—See Life of the Saint by Ratisbonne.

Oh let thy penance, like his, be true,
Heartfelt, and deep, and abiding too!
So mayst thou, like St. Thais, see
The throne of a seraph reserved for thee.

Remember Him who, with zeal untold,
The little ones chose as the purest gold
To burnish for heaven, and set in them
Devotion, charity's brightest gem;
And who unwearied, in robe of power,
Sat from the dawn until night's calm hour,
Loosing the bonds from the burdened soul
Where nature bent beneath faith's control.

And, oh, remember at eventide
How good and penitent side by side
Wreath'd the same garland St. Dominic wove,
Centuries since, for the queen of love;
All gladly offering praise and prayer
To the Lily of Israel, fair all fair,
The glory of earth, the beloved of God,
The root of the flower of Jesse's rod.

Remember the dedication made,
And at her feet with such full heart laid,
Of mind and body, and soul and heart,
Of all that thou hopest, or hast or art.
And the prayers then breath'd for the loved and few
Friends of thy bosom, the tried, the true,
That as over Colmar,* o'er thee and thine
The marks of her power and love may shine.

---

* In allusion to an anecdote told by one of the Fathers.

Remember the promises made aloud
In the sacred church 'mid the witness crowd,
While the guardian spirits on pinions bright
Wafted the words to the realms of light:
"In God my Creator I do believe,
And His teachings through holy Cnurch receive,
And against Satan and sin engage
A war that shall end but with life to wage."

There was joy in the heavens that blessed night,
Angels in rapture beheld the sight
Of all those white robes again made clean
In the blood of the Man-God, the Nazarene.
Treasure the blessings thou gainedst then,
Thou ne'er may'st be granted such grace again;
Cease not to pray lest another brow
Be decked with the crown for thee destined now.

Remember "the Fathers." for thou shalt meet
Those faces again at the judgment seat.
Shall they witness for thee? Oh shall they tell
That thou hast remembered the mission well?
That the robe of thy baptism pure and white
And unstained thou hast kept since that solemn night?
Or, like the friend of Elpiphadore,
Shall they uphold it the Judge before?

Merciful Father, who dost forget
The sins of the penitent, never let
The child of Thy handmaid betray the trust
Thou hast confided to such frail dust.
Grant that in safety at Jesus' feet,
All that I love may in glory meet—
Life ebbeth quickly, but, O my Queen!
My soul 'neath the folds of thy mantle screen.

HOME MEMORIES.

Summer, bright summer, thou'rt come again,
Gladdening the hearts and the homes of men,
Filling the earth with the beauty bright
Which at thy coming hath sprung to light;
Even in the city all brick and stone
Thou as a welcome guest art known.
But I love thee most in the country where
Every thing doth in thy bounty share,
Where hill and valley, and grove and dell
Burst into beauty at thy bright spell.

Summer, bright summer, how you and I
Sported together in days gone by!
When every flower and bush and bird
Was familiar to me as a household word,
And thou didst strew o'er my own green land
The choicest gifts of thy fairy hand.
Ah, sadly my spirit turneth back
The steps of those pleasant times to track,
For many a bitter change hath come
Since I shared in the glee of the wild bee's hum.

And I dwell again in my childhood's home,
And over its fields of blossoms roam,
And the gentle primrose hath bloomed again,
And the daisies are strewed o'er the grass like rain;
And the flowery hawthorn its fragrance blends
With the odor sweet of its humbler friends,
While the woodbine beareth her perfumed store
To fill her place when the day is o'er;
And the magpie has built in the old ash tree,
And every thing looks as of old to me.

And I see the spot where the angry jay
Scared me from pulling May flowers away,
For I had intruded too near her nest,
And she loudly resented her broken rest.
So the doors were left on that fair May eve
Without half the flowers I used to leave
To quell the anger of witch or fay
That might before morning pass that way:
'Twas an offering children loved to make
Just for the flower-gathering's sake.

And the graceful tree with its showers of gold,
Where the pretty chaffinch her partner told
How the leafy Savan gave ample shade
Where their nest might be with all safety made;
While the green linnet chose the evergreen oak
To hide her young from the magpie's stroke,
And the blackbird sung sweetly above its nest
As if lulling its little ones to rest,
Or proudly poured from its golden beak
The praises that we so faintly speak.

And there is the well known holly-bush,
The chosen home of the tuneful thrush,
The bird that my father loved so well,
And whose welcome note on his quick ear fell
As at the brake of each bright day-dawn
It pealed over garden and court and lawn,
Winning him back to the happy hours
When his heart was pure as the dew-decked flowers,
And filling his sick room, like words of love
From those who are gone to their home above.

But the thrush sings now to a stranger ear,
No voices of home in its halls I hear,

And the lily-fringed lake so calm and blue,
Hath passed to the hands of the stranger too;
In the old chapel, below the hill,
Void is *our* place, that none else may fill.
But many a look of fond regret
Is turned to that side of the altar yet,
And many a fervent and heartfelt prayer,
Is breathed for those who of old knelt there.

Lord of the seasons, to Thee I bow,
Though my heart in its loneness yearneth now
For the happy home of my life's young morn,
Whose roses as yet deeply hid each thorn;
For the pleasant scenes of my childish play,
And of graver joys at a later day,
When my spirit woke to the awful sense
Of Thine own beauty, untold, immense,
And learned in Thy creatures on Thee to look,
And to hear Thy voice in each murmuring brook.

ROSARY SUNDAY.

On this sweet solemnity
I will twine a wreath for thee,
Solace of the exile's heart,
Mary! of my life a part.
Look not on my sinfulness,
But my will to make it less,
Bless the efforts of thy child,
Guide her thro' life's dang'rous wild,
And accept this coronal,
From a heart that loves thee well—
White, and red, and golden-hued
Are the blossoms 'round me strew'd.

From the first bright flowers of spring
To the last on summer's wing,
I will choose each fairest gem
For my Lady's diadem.
Purest snowdrop whose fair head
Bendeth o'er her grassy bed;
Primrose smiling thro' bright tears
When the sun-shower disappears,
And the daisy shining ever
By each bank and brae and river,
Canovan of wavy plume,
Blush rose of the sweet perfume,
Narcissus of beauty bright,
And the rocket richly white,
And the lily of the vale,
And the lotus-flower pale,
And the snowy Guelder rose,
And the tiny flower that grows
On the shamrock, chosen sign
Of the Trinity Divine.—
These shall speak of joy to thee
Borne in the mystery
Of the Incarnation, when
Jesus came to dwell with men;
Of the greeting which St. John
Offered to thy holy Son,
When thou borest Him to bless
Hebron, thro' thy lowliness,
In that of His humble birth
When the angels bore to earth
Tidings of the highest joy,
And proclaimed the infant Boy,
Meekly nestling in thy breast,
He in whom man should be blest;
And of that pure offering
Thou didst to the temple bring!

Priceless gift, which thou alone
Worthily could'st call thine own.
They shall represent the gladness
Which gave place to the deep sadness,
By the absence of thy Child,
On thy gentle bosom piled,
Till thou found'st Him meekly teaching
Truths beyond poor reason's reaching.
In my garland next I'll twine
The rich crimson columbine
With Damascus roses, and
Blossoms of the tulip grand,
And geranium, brilliant flower,
And the fuchsia's graceful shower.
"Love lies bleeding," too, shall pour
Her sad grace this chaplet o'er;
For, alas! these symbolize
All the blood and tears and sighs
In the sad Gethsemane
By thy Son outpoured for me;
And the scourging which He bore
All the jeering crowd before,
And the thorn crown that pressed
On the head so oft caressed
By thy gentle hand, which now
Cannot wipe His bleeding brow;
And the painful journey made
With the cross upon Him laid,
Sinking, 'neath the fearful load
Of our sins, upon the road;
And the blood that all around
Sprinkled Calvary's sacred mound,
All the precious drops that fell
O'er the form He loved so well.
Lady, wilt thou not obtain,
That for me they be not vain?—

Of the golden Daffodil
Freshly gathered from the hill,
And the fragrant cowslips springing
Where the silver streams are singing,
And the clusters softly flung,
O'er laburnum branches young,
And the starry buttercup
Thro' its green leaves twinkling up,
And the crocus brightly glowing
Where the sunbeams down are flowing.—
Now shall be my wreath, for they
Speak of sufferings passed away;
Tell how Jesus rose again
On that blessed morning, when
To the women He made known,
Thro' that sweet name of thine own,
That in risen glory He
Now from death's dark bonds was free,
And converted all their sorrow
Into joy, that cannot borrow
Simile from aught we know
Of rejoicing here below.
May that name us also bring
To the presence of our King!
Tell us how on Olivet
For a while He lingered yet,
And then blessing thee and those
Who were with thee, as He rose,
Left thee filled with consolation
For the work of man's salvation;
For the thought that now thy Son
Shall no more be spat upon,
But that in his glory He
Shall throughout eternity
Reign the Lord of life and light,
King of mercy as of might.

Of the Holy Spirit, too,
Speak these flowers of golden hue;
Of the love with which He came
In those brilliant tongues of flame,
And the graces which He gave
To those sent the world to save.
But could aught to thee be given,
Worthy Queen of earth and heaven?
Could that purest heart find place
For more large or ample grace?
No, sweet Mother!—Then restore
Us our portion, we implore;
Thou hast found what we have lost,
On this stormy ocean tossed.
Thy Assumption, too, they speak,
Virgin ever mild and meek,
For thy Son would not allow
Stain upon thy spotless brow,
Nor corruption e'er to come
To that bosom once His home.
And of angel bands who haste
Of thy presence sweet to taste,
Of their joy that on that day
All thy sufferings passed away;
Thou wert seated on a throne
Worthy thee and thee alone.
Now are mortals filled with hope,
For they know thy hand will ope
Ever to the needy, who
Call upon your Son thro' you,
Treasures from thy heart divine,
Given for such souls as mine.
Glory be unto that Son
While the endless ages run!
Glory to the Father be
Who refuses naught to thee!

Glory to the Holy Ghost,
And to those who love thee most!
Grace and peace and blessing be
Now and through Eternity!   Amen,

OH TAKE ME, MARY.*

LOWLY he lay; a burning fever o'er him
  Had flung its heavy arms, and in his brain
Were shadows of strange things, and thoughts that bore
    him
  Back to his home and made him see again
Faces and scenes beloved—and then they rested
  Upon what filled his inmost soul with love,
The Virgin's altar: and his words attested
  How far his heart was this poor world above.

And thus he spoke: "Mary, my heart is burning
  With its desire to go to thee, my Queen,
It sighs for that blest home whence no returning
  Is ever, ever to life's changeful seene;
There thou art reigning in supernal brightness
  On His right hand, thy God, and yet thy Son.
Lily of fadeless, of all spotless whiteness,
  When shall my exile on this earth be done?
                    Oh take me, Mary.

"Take me hence, Mary, let me see thy glory,
  Breathe but the wish and I shall be set free;
Or as thy holy servant, Saint Liguori,
  Taught me to hope, come bear me hence with thee.

---

* These lines were suggested to the writer by hearing of the constant
aspiration of a dear reverend friend, now bishop of her native diocese, during
a severe illness in St. Vincent's Hospital.

And while around me those earth-angels hover
  Breathing of Heaven, though still laboring here,
Let me depart, forbid that I recover,
  Life and not death I look upon with fear!
                    Oh take me, Mary.

"Yes, take me, Mary, while thus far apart
  From those who joyed with me in life's young morning,
Take me, but soothe, oh soothe my father's heart,
  For the fair flower his latest years adorning.
The old man glories that his boy before thee
  Offers to God the sacrifice so dread:
Hope of the hopeless, soothe him, I implore thee,
  When I am numbered with the silent dead,
                    And take me, Mary.

"And there is one—would that he now were near me,
  Thou knowest him well, my friend, my more than
      brother;
Oft as I breathe his name, he may not hear me,
  Wilt thou not bless him for my sake, sweet Mother?
My sister who hath known no mother's teaching,
  No mother's love, oh let her find in thee
A guide, a Mother; let thy hand, outreaching,
  Lead her to Heaven to kiss thy feet with me,
                    And take me, Mary.

"Bless the good Sisters, make them worthy daughters
  Of their great founder, glorious de Paul,
Guide them thyself o'er life's tempestuous waters,
  Be kind to them, as they are kind to all.
And when in turn they too are lowly lying,
  Then let them feel thy more than mother's love;
Oh let them know no bitterness in dying,
  But pass in triumph to their home above,
                    And take them, Mary."

TO OUR BLESSED LADY.

MARY, my Queen, my Mother dear!
Behold me at thy feet,
Oh deign thy servant's heart to cheer
And teach me what is meet
For me to do to honor thee,
And best to serve thy Son:
Obtain, sweet Lady, that in me
At least thy will be done.

Thou knowest well this heart of mine
It hides no thought from thee,
Oh Mary ! make it wholly thine,
And from all passion free,
And may thy Son, for thy dear sake,
Pardon my every crime,
And the last remnant deign to take
Of my long misspent time.

Alas ! alas ! that youth's bright years
All fruitlessly have sped,
As fall the leaves the lightning sears
E'er yet their spring is fled.
But may the future by thy aid
Atone for all the past;
My every care on thee is laid,
Oh save me at the last!

COME HOME.

COME home, my brother, home—
Far o'er the ocean's foam
He comes, the gentle-hearted,
From us and thee long parted,

The sharer of thy joy
When thou wert but a boy.

'Tis he! yes, 'tis the same,
Thy partner in the game
Of bat and ball and "scout" *
When burst the schoolboys out
In wild exultant glee,
Of care and study free.

'Tis he who stayed behind,
In our own land to find
Saving and sacred lore
Laid up, as in its store;
And now hath come to share
The exiled people's care.

Come home! Oh haste that we
May gaze on him and thee,
As in the bright days when
The cares of busy men
Were lesser in our eyes
Than summer butterflies.

Come home! I bid thee not
Seek out the sacred spot,
Watered by sunny rills,
Amid green Ulster's hills,
Where in true hearts' deep love
And memory still we move.

I do not bid thee sail,
To sea-girt Innisfail,

---

* A manly game, much loved by boys in Ireland.

For thou wouldst but have sped
To mourn as of the dead,
Thy mother of whose breast
Thou wert beloved the best.

Whose gentle hand and voice
'Mid all the world's noise,
Seems still to guide and bless
Us in our loneliness;
Oh may we worthy be
Of her blest memory!

Thy father, he who bowed
Him never to the proud
Serfs of a foreign land,
But ever took his stand
On the down-trodden side,
Till he was crushed, and died.

There, where O'Donnell Roe,
Escaping from the foe,
Found shelter in the free
Home of thy sires and thee,
While the six princes kept
Armed vigil while he slept.

In Truagh's majestic woods
And by the Blackwater's floods,
Still doth thy race remain;
And in the sweet refrain
Of song and legend old,
Fondly their deeds are told.

Oh 'twere too sad that thou
Shouldst see thy old home now,

But still its spirit dwells,
With all its sacred spells,
Where *kindred* hearts are found,
Tho' all be *strange* around.

Thy brother comes, but strange
And awful is the change
In him, since last with you
He coursed the green fields through:
In that fair brow serene,
A seal hath planted been.

He hath girt on the sword
Of Gideon and the Lord,
To shield the stricken ones,
Of our own land the sons;
To succor, guard, and guide
The souls for whom Christ died.

Now 'tis his place to stand
Between the people and
Their God, who in His love
Descended from above,
Bearing rich gifts to all
Who on His mercy call.

Come home ! that we may kneel
And those beloved hands feel
In blessing o'er each head
Of all the household spread,
And bless the Lord who thus
Hath deigned to comfort us.

TO MARIE.

DEAR friend unseen, unknown,
What charm is round us thrown
That thus attracteth kindred heart to heart,
That thus our joy to thee
A fount of bliss should be,
And in our blessedness thou shouldst have part?

The music of our land
Martial, or gay, or grand,
All hath a taint of sadness in its tone;
Thus hath our gathered joy
A sad yet sweet alloy,
For one, our chosen one, for aye is gone.

Yes she who sung "come home,"
But to the exile's home,
Already hath she left it, she is gone;
Before the altar now,
Or where worn sufferers bow,
She standeth with *new* sisters, yet alone.

Alone, and for His sake
Who would our nature take,
Leaving the glories of His heavenly home,
Like Him to tend the poor,
And plaintless to endure
All that of sorrow or distress may come.

'Tis but in spirit now
Together we may bow,
Before the shrine of shrines, the saint of saints,
And thou, Marie, for me
Oh let your pleading be,
For in this loneliness my sad heart faints.

7*

Oh thankless, dull, and cold
The heart that is not bold
All suffering to suffer for His sake!
Why should we feel alone
While to His hidden throne,
The burdens of our sorrow we may take?

There pour out all our grief,
There learn to make the chief
Sorrow and passion of our inmost heart,
To see our God denied,
Forgotten, cast aside,
And know that in this work we have had part.

Away, away the cares
Of earth, they are but snares
Twining around to keep our hearts from this,
Their one dear work below,
Incense to make and throw
For ever on His shrine who only is.

And while the dread years flee
Let us be friends, though we
Strangers in earth's dull common sense may be:
Have I not seen you bow
Before the bleeding brow
Of Him thus agonized for you, for me?

TO OUR BLESSED LADY.

On thy natal-day, sweet Mother,
Bless me, take me, to thy heart
And from out thy loving guidance
Let me never more depart.

Lead me close to thee, my Mother,
 Not through paths of fragrant flowers;
Teach my wayward will to follow
 Thee in life's all-darkened hours.

By that life so sadly stricken
 Through thy Son's with sins of mine,
Give me grace to drain the chalice
 By the memory of thine.

Help me, Mary, make me faithful
 Ever His dear law to keep;
And to thee, my own loved Mother,
 Nearer let my spirit leap.

Help all those I love so dearly,
 Lend us all thine aid, so sweet
Through this life, and hear our heart-prayer,
 That in heaven "we all may meet."

THANKS!

Jesus, my Lord, my God!
 I meekly bow
Beneath Thy chastening rod,
 And thank Thee *now*
That Thou hast crushed life's longings all to dust,
Bidding my heart in Thee alone to trust.

Jesus! I ask but strength
 The storm to brave;
Ah! with Thy saving love
 My spirit lave—
Save me thro' this, the bitterest of all
The sorrows that upon me now could fall.

Jesus! I offer Thee
A broken chain,
Whose links are scattered
O'er a tideless main
Broken and useless; once so bright, they lie
Trophies of hopes long dead—that *still* rush by.

Jesus! the struggle's past—
One boon I crave,
Rescue this blinded soul
From life's dread grave;
Rescue and purify—through cruel pain
Make her seek Thy dear Heart—Thy child again.

ADESTE FIDELES.

GRATEFUL hearts their incense bringing,
Angel-choirs their sweet notes singing,
Sad, low tones are softly ringing
            Glory to God on high.
Heaven to earth its joy is lending,
Fervent prayers are faintly blending,
With angelic hosts ascending
            Far beyond the sky.

Fraught with pain, sad bells are pealing,
Pain no tender love concealing;
Joy, the Infant's birth revealing,
            With the sadness reigns.
For He comes--no monarch's throne
Waits Him—ever poor and lone
As His prophets had foreshown,
            For us He deigns

To suffer.   At His first drawn breath
He sees and knows the life of death,
And bows the heavy cross beneath
                    His Baby-Heart.
Jesus! 'tis thus, though King of kings,
A chime of joy and sadness rings,
As to Thy crib each wanderer brings
                    Longings apart.

Sorrow—for Thee, O Saviour dear!
Joy—for Thy children struggling here;
Brought by Thy Heart's deep love so near
                    The gates of peace.
Infant, all gentle, mild, and sweet!
We place in homage at Thy feet
Our hearts, whose love though incomplete
                    Shall never cease.

GLORIA IN EXCELSIS DEO!

GLORIA in excelsis Deo!
  Christmas chimes, are heard again,
And the angels leave their white thrones,
  With God's holiest "peace to men"—
Humbly soars their deep heart-worship
  As the joyous praises ring,
For they bear to earth "glad tidings"
  Of the new-born Infant King.

Let us watch their gentle hovering
  O'er the shepherds whom they lead,
Through untrodden paths in midnight
  On to Bethlehem they speed.

And they rest them in a stable!
  Where the oxen keep Him warm,
While all within that little town
  Are sheltered from the storm.

Ah! He's looking down so sweetly
  O'er each heart these Christmas days,
Waiting for its love and worship,
  For its smallest mite of praise.
Let us strive to be His children,
  In His suffering if we share,
One bright day above in heaven,
  We with Him our crowns shall wear.

PASSION WEEK.

Passion Week! its dreadful mysteries
  Fill the heart with anxious care,
And the spirit's love is brooding,
  O'er the Saviour's lonely prayer.

In Gethsemane behold Him,
  Anguish steals His blood away,
Hear Him ask His heavenly Father
  These last earthly hours to stay.

Know our sins have scourged with scourging,
  Like to which none e'er was known;
Know, our selfish hearts have goaded,
  As our hearts could goad alone.

Know His heart so aches to love us,
  That 'tis crushed with bitter pain,
Yet He opens all its channels
  To receive His sheep again.

And this love we will not give Him,
  Trifling, worthless though it be,
While He thirsts e'en for one whisper,
  That shall sound eternally.

Thirsts to see us truly sorrowing
  O'er the work which is our own,
Longs to see our weak hearts burning,
  In His love courageous grown.

Jesus! Lord! we long to love thee,
  And we long thy cross to bear,
Give us, Lord, our destined portion,
  Let us in Thy passion share.

Crucify our hearts, Lord Jesus,
  Till they bow in anguish meet,
Purified, made fit to serve Thee,
  Sanctified, our love complete.

And when we have drained the chalice,
  Trod the way to Calvary's height,
Blend our aching hearts together,
  Then to share the same delight.

Then to kneel in love before Thee,
  Chanting evermore Thy praise,
In Thine own majestic presence,
  Free, dear Lord, on Thee to gaze.

TO OUR LADY OF SORROWS.

MATER Dolorosa! be my Mother now,
In tears and sorrow at thy feet I humbly bow,
And ask thine aid life's every pang to bear
It is but meet that with thee I should share
                    Thy weight of woe.

Shield me! the tempest winds blow fierce and cold—
Save me! lest I should stray from His dear fold,
Where suffering borne for Him, with thee, is blest,
E'en though the heart *must* bleed, for me 'tis best.
     Dost thou not know,

Dost thou not see the struggle? Stay the tears,
Upholding, by the memory of the years
In which thine eyes were dim, thy heart all sore,
For every thorn of His pierced thee still more—
     And led thee on,

On to the heights where all His love was shed
For souls so wilful. When those words He said
That made me even *then*, thine own, thy child,
Did'st thou not claim this heart, so proud and wild,
     From Him, thy Son?

Mother of Sorrows! claim me now, as then,
And take me to thy heart of hearts again,
Do not reject these wandering words I pray—
Remember, that I must be thine to-day,
     And thine alone.

Sorrowing Heart! shed o'er my life thy grace
And welcome me in suffering's fond embrace,
Bind to the Cross this shrinking soul and bless
The heart that thirsts for love and tenderness,
     Beneath thy throne.

COME UNTO ME, ALL YE WHO LABOR.

Come unto Me! I am thy Lord! thy Saviour!
 Come! when the cross o'erpowers thy feeble heart,
Come! and remember that in all thy sorrows
 Before thou wert I bore the sadder part.

Let not thy soul, despairing 'neath its burden,
 Give up the task allotted to be done
In its short life—remember that in suffering
 Alone 'tis sanctified—its goal is won.

Hast thou grown tired? Come, refresh thy spirit
 In the cool waters of My boundless love,
Where in the placid streamlets are reflected
 The beauties of the starry sky above.
Come, with thy every thought, thy whole strength turning
 Unto the Heart that folds thee close within,
That Heart so pierced will each endeavor cherish,
 Will guide thee safely through a world of sin.

Come unto Me! and heal thy heart-wounds bleeding;
 Come then and fear not, give to Me thy pain,
If thou wilt lay the cross from off thy shoulders
 Remember—I must take it up again.
Come unto Me! have I not proved—how truly!—
 My love for thee—was not My life-blood shed
For thee, for thee alone, who would'st reject Me,
 And place fresh thorns around My aching head?

Come! let Me bind thee to thy cross and shrink not—
 He who gives all, shall all in turn receive—
Have I not promised this unto My children?
 Thou knowest that thy Lord cannot deceive.
Come unto Me! My yoke is full of sweetness,
 Brightly the roses with the thorns are strewn,
And angel-hearts await thee at the summit
 Of Calvary's mount to claim thee as their own.

"SIMPLY TO THY CROSS I CLING."

JESUS Saviour, Lord Divine!
Let my heart to Thee incline—
Louder let the anthem ring,
"Simply to Thy cross I cling."

Let it lead me on to Thee
Over life's all-stormy sea,
Jesus, Master, Lord and King!
"Simply to Thy Cross I cling."

Saviour of this thankless child,
Heart so tired and sin-defiled,
Mercy show through every sting—
"Simply to Thy Cross I cling."

Let me kneel for ever there,
At its foot, in heartfelt prayer,
With the poor, weak love I bring,
Let me to Thy dear Cross cling.

PRAYER.

JESUS! agonizing, dying,
Humbled, sad, forsaken, lone,
By the depths of bitter sorrow
That my sins have o'er thee thrown—

Jesus! Jesus! hear me, love me,
Make me fit to be Thy bride,
Let me drink the healing waters
Flowing from Thy sacred side.

Jesus! Saviour! make me humble,
Let me Thee in all things seek,
I would be a willing victim,
But, dear Lord, my heart is weak.

Give me faith, strength, courage, Saviour,
Loose the bonds that bind so fast;
Thou alone canst free me, Jesus,
From the sad thoughts of the past.

Let my heart be Thine, Thine only,
Though too full of stain to praise—
Thine for ever, Saviour Jesus!
Brought to Thee "through divers ways."

"TAKE THESE THINGS HENCE."

"Take these things hence!"–Oh take them all, dear Jesus,
This pride so haughty and self-love supreme,
That shut my soul from out Thy beauteous vision
And leave life's noblest purposes a dream.

"Take these things hence!"—Am I to be Thy servant,
And love Thee not upon Thy thorny way—
Am I to be Thy child, nay more, Thy handmaid,
And leave Thy chalice flowing day by day?

Shall I not drain it willingly and deeply,
And bear the cross which on Thee I have lain
Too often, in the years which Thou hast given
And I have lost, to free my soul from stain?

"Take these things hence," and purify my being,
Lose not the Precious Blood which Thou hast shed
To save my soul, to weave my crown in heaven,
Are all the heart-strings of my spirit dead.

"Take these things hence!" Take Thou myself, dear Jesus,
And let the future years blot out the past,
That through Thy Sacred Heart, my poor life giving,
I may be counted worthy of going *home*, at last.

RESURREXIT !

Resurrexit! Resurrexit!
In triumphant glory now,
Gone the cross that pained Thy shoulder,
And the thorns that pierced Thy brow.

Gone! a crown of heavenly lustre
Dazzles our poor, mortal eyes,
Lord! in mercy hear the anthems
That from every heart arise.

Resurrexit! Resurrexit!
Open wide, O heavenly gate!—
For His rescued, chosen army,
Quick! the angels longing wait.

Vainly Magdalena seeks Thee—
"He thou seekest is not here:"
Such the answer to her questioning—
Angels bid her not to fear,

Tell her that her Lord has risen,
And she turns so sad away,
When she hears a voice call "Mary!"
One word, "Master," does she say.

How He soothes His dear apostles—
"Ever with thee, will I be,"
Preach thou everywhere *My* preaching,
Say what *I* have said to thee.

I have loved thee—still I love thee,
Ah! how dear, *thou* canst not tell,
Now, I go to send the spirit:
To His maxims listen well.

Resurrexit ! Resurrexit !
  Lord, dear Lord! we seek Thee too—
Let not all our search be hopeless,
  With that dazzling crown in view.

Let us, when Thy summons calleth,
  Rise triumphant unto Thee;
Until then, dear Lord, enchain us
  In Thy boundless charity.

"EXULTEMUS !"

THESE blessed hours ! these blessed hours !
  This glorious Easter Day
Countless the gifts of love I ask,
  Silent the words I say.

And as the "Exultemus" thrills
  Each fibre of my heart,
The old "Hæc Dies" wakes old chords,
  The hot tears burning start.

Hosanna ! Alleluia ! Lord!
  With grace my heart imbue,
With love and mercy fill it o'er
  Till it pulsate anew.

Anew ! invigorated ! firm !
  These are the boons I crave
To spend this lifetime but for Thee,
  For Thee all storms to brave.

Let these old Alleluias ring
  For ever through my soul,
And bring me back these Easter days,
  And all my life control.

SAINT AUGUSTINE.

A KNEELING Mother prayed and wept,
Grief to her heart had closely crept;
And bowed before God's holy shrine,
She murmured, "Thy dear will—not mine."
To cheer my soul, O Jesus! send one ray,
This anguish fierce in mercy stay—
Mary, my Mother! on thee too I call,
Save him, my only boy, my life, my all!
Save him, for whom thine own dear Son hath died,
Save him in memory of that bleeding side—
Save him in memory of thy years of grief,
Oh let this wilful life of his be brief.
Thy holy name in love he whispers not—
Oh must *his childish grace be all forgot?*—
Hours passed, and still, as only woman would,
She *prayed and wept as but a mother could.*

Years had gone by, and still this child of prayer
In all the pleasures of this world held share,
Scoffed at his Maker, His sweet name reviled—
The mother's prayer grew louder for her child.
Nature had given him charms—the rarest kind —
Richer by far, the graces of his mind,
Glowing with eloquence, he thousands swayed—
In sweeter accents still the mother prayed.

The setting sun sinks slowly,
    Still there lingers one stray beam
Gilding each mossy ruined tower
    Bath'd in each rippling stream.
The Vesper-bell peals softly,
    And the church's aisles are filled,
The priest is in the pulpit
    And the noisy throng is stilled.

He speaks—and all the wondering, awe-struck crowd,
Kneel down and worship 'neath that altar bowed,
And see in spirit Calvary's dismal height
Imbued in darkness deadlier than the night.
They see that form, and know that they have hung
Their Lord and Saviour, and their hearts are wrung
With grief; they count the wounds made by those nails
And e'en the hardest 'neath the vision pales.
They see the thorny crown pressed on His head,
And know that for their sake their God has bled;
They place their hands the wounded side within,
And feel the tenfold weight of every sin.
They hear His own sweet, loving voice, so true,
"Father, forgive—they know not what they do!"
They see the Virgin clinging to the cross,—
Her Son alone can know her fearful loss;
While to her bleeding heart He gives the care
Of all who in this dreadful crime have share.
They *see* the light'ning, hear the thunder roll,
And sunk in bitter grief is every soul
Of that vast throng who hunger for each word,
Spoken by this true servant of the Lord.
He leads them onward still, to heaven's gate,
And shows to them their happy future fate,
If faithful they in every word and deed
Turn to our Mother in each hour of need.
He tells them how they never can be saved,
Unless in healing waters they are laved;
And tells them, too, how this dear, loving Son,
If brave they battle till the victory's won,
Will say—"Thy work fulfilled, now come with Me,
Unto My Father's mansions thou art free!

Thousands repented of their lives that night,
Deep in their souls had shone a wondrous light,

And many hardened sinners humbly knelt,
Revealed their woes, more peace and comfort felt
Than had been theirs for years; and thus they knew
The words that he had spoken must be true.

Who *was* this man to whom was given the power
Of holding all so spell-bound hour by hour,
Of bringing wanderers home unto that goal.
Where love and mercy re-baptize the soul ?
That kneeling mother's prayers high heaven had reached
And now her noble son the Gospel preached.
His lofty mind, ambitious heart, were bent
In reparation for the years misspent.
A mother's love had *saved* the tempest-tossed—
Her life-long fervent prayers, could not be lost—
And never in God's Holy Church was seen
A greater, nobler Saint than AUGUSTINE.

"SOLVE VINCLA REIS."

BINDING thy heart, my darling,
   Wilt thou not break them all ?
Fly from this midnight darkness—
   Darker than death's dread pall.
Canst thou not *humbly* offer
   All at thy Saviour's feet,
Loosen the bonds that keep thee
   Far from His love so sweet ?

Solve! these chains so mighty
   Fill all thy life with fear,
Cast away all these shackles,—
   "*Love* alone reigneth here."

Spouse of the Lord, remember
Short is this life, a dream
That passeth, returning never
From out time's mystic stream.

And wilt thou lose the treasure
Held to thy raptured gaze?
Lose it for tears and sufferings?
Dim all its beauteous rays?
Pray to our Mother, Mary,
Bid her these chains to break,
Count not the cost, my darling,
'Tis for our Lord's dear sake.

Fetter Him not in sorrow,
Crown not that brow anew,
Love him and serve *Him* bravely
His love is *not* untrue.
Break all "these captive fetters,"
Work out thy destined part,
Mary will shed such sunbeams
Into thy aching heart.

Yes, she will love and guard thee,
Her prayers can never fail,
And she will lead thee safely
Far from this "weary vale."
And smiles will adorn thee, darling,
And sorrow shall fade away,
And pass from this awful midnight
Into God's glorious day.

RETRIBUTION.

At the Book of Life an angel stands
        With drooping wings,
Watching in awe the quick-flowing sands
        When a loud toll rings.
The pages fall from his trembling hands,
The hour has come !—and the Lord demands
The soul he has led through life's sinking strands
        To eternal springs.

He turns to his record—a leaf, the first, ·
        Meets his wistful gaze,
He had guarded that soul when no taint accursed
        Marred its earlier days.
Those days are past and their graces lost,
Vainly he'd anchor the tempest-tossed
In peace, but that life-line in *black* is crossed,
        Cast from its Maker's praise.

He veils in those white wings that sun-lit face,
        For a ray appears,
Revealing treasures of squandered grace—
        And the angel's tears
Flow in anguished love, but cannot efface
The past, and this spirit must lose its place.
Vainly he seeks for one saving trace
        Through life's dreadful years.

Sadly he closes the last page down
        While he humbly prays:
Mary ! thy love may regain this crown
        And love's beauteous rays.
Illumine his soul! is it true—can it be,
The margin is golden, that soul may see
Thy heavenly home, and again be free
        In those nightless days ?

The bell ceased its tolling—the angel blessed
His Lord's dearest bounty, and then caressed
The weary child who had wandered far
From Bethlehem's crib and the Magi's star;
And the lost crown, by his prayer re-won,
With more than resplendent beauty shone,—
Shone through His dear wounds on Calvary,
Poor wandering pilgrim—and all for thee.

PARTINGS.

MERCILESSLY, onward, rushing,
　Wrenching with a force so dread
Heart from kindred heart for ever,
　From which years of life have fled;
Bleeding, crushing, wounded, dying—
Can aught heal a lone heart's sighing?

Brother, sisters, home's *dear* circle
　In life's earlier hours complete,
Torn by will, unseen, relentless,
　That no mortal dare defeat:
How we live in anguish, hiding
Heart-wounds from all harsh deriding.

Courage! life with all its miseries
　Draws full quickly towards the hour
When shall cease this fearful turmoil,
　When shall shine God's wondrous power.
At His throne again united,
Radiant grown the hopes now blighted.

Clasped in fond embraces, never
    To be torn apart again,
And to know how angels ever
    Treasured crowns for every pain.
And our Mother's love shall meet us,
Where our Lord shall stoop to greet us.

No more ceaseless sorrow wailing
    Sheltered in that Sacred Heart,
Which e'en now longs to receive us,
    And to heal the poisoned dart.
Saviour! Saviour! give us grace,
All thy footsteps to retrace,
And unite us, God of love,
In Thy beauteous courts above,
Where these crushing griefs shall end,
And heart press heart, and friend meet friend.

"WHATEVER IS, IS RIGHT."

"WHATEVER is, is right,"—poor human heart, awaken
    Unto the love that bears thy pain on high,
And totter not beneath the blow uplifted,
    Look to God's grace, illumining life's sky.

"Whatever is, is right," and best, and truest,
    Token unseen of His most tender care,
Who, that His joy our souls may know in Heaven,
    Sends us—sweet gift!—His passion here to share.

"Whatever is, is right,"—ah! well thou knowest:
    Wherefore this sinking down of heart and mind
If from thy life *one* light hath passed *for ever?*
    Search deep, far brighter is the lamp thou'lt find.

"Whatever is, is right,"—graces abundant
Shall flow, wherever grief has purified
The stains which on thy untamed heart were branded
When thou wouldst fly from Jesus crucified.

"Whatever is, is right,"—suffer in silence—
Jesus has suffered silently for thee,
Give with a loving, tender will—remember,
Sorrow shall cease, but not eternity.

A BLESSING.

"Good-night! God bless you, darling,"—
  Back through life's saddened haze,
Its sweeter echoes woo me,
  But the tear-drops dim my gaze;
For a soft low voice is stilling
  My young hot heart to rest,
Loving arms close fast around me,
  And the sobs *are* half-suppressed.

"Good-night! God bless you, darling,"
  And a gentle hand is lain,
With its blessed touch all soothing
  O'er a weight of childish pain.
Yes! I *was* a child but dreaming—
  Passionate and proud and wild,
Dreaming ever as the moments
  Sped and left me—not a child.

How I chafed beneath the present,
  Longing that its days were past,
Conjured up a cloudless future,
  Over which no shade should cast

Sorrow—no! 'twas *ever* peopled
  With the hearts I loved so well;
Should hope fade and cold grey shadows
  Ever break this childish spell?

"Good-night! God bless you, darling!"
  How the years had sped away—
But the same dear nightly greeting
  Ever closed each checkered day.
Yes! the years had flown, and found me
  Passionate, and wild, and proud;
All the childish hopes *had* vanished,
  Neath life's grey and leaden cloud.

"Good-night! God bless my darling!"
  How those soft sweet echoes thrill
Through my inmost heart, with memories
  Of the old days mingling still
With *all* life held of gladness
  In those hours of early joy,
When one heart held *all* our sorrows,
  Which its love would fain destroy.

"Good-night! God bless you, darling,"
  And the dear lips closed to mine—
Dearer words were *never* spoken,
  Never voice, nor heart like thine.
But 'tis *past*—I may not hear them
  Now, strange blessings ever greet
The child whose haughty sorrows
  Ever heard thy voice so sweet,

Ever knew thy greeting failed not,
  Ever felt thy sheltering love.
Mother! mother! gentlest, dearest,
  Will one home be ours above?

Will those blessed words, my mother,
  Shield the child so far away,
Will they bless her *now* that from thee,
  In *strange paths* her footsteps stray?

THOUGHTS BY THE SEASIDE.

How I love the grand old ocean,
  Stretching blue from shore to shore,
With its wild untaméd motion,
  And its deep melodious roar.
I love it *best* when angry,
  Like my own heart throbbing wild,
And I love it, too, when quiet,
  Playful, as a little child.

What a horde of untold suffering
  Neath its bosom seeks for rest,
And how many a homeless wanderer
  Have those cold, dark billows pressed.
How it speaks of power supernal!
  What a lesson does it preach!
How it bids us live in trembling
  That our destined home we'll reach!

And though fierce is this wild ocean,
  What—the ocean of our hearts,
Which bears us on all heedless
  Of the love which grace imparts.
Like the little streamlets flowing,
  Far away their fountain head:
So do we in reckless moments
  Fly from Him who for us bled.

Yes, dear Lord, we wander blindly
    From the ocean of Thy grace,
Not the sorrows of a lifetime
    Can our many sins efface.
Yet we know Thy mercy, Saviour!
    And You know our hearts are weak:
So in Thy most gracious accents
    Bid us love and pardon seek.

And we know Thy yoke is sweeter,
    And Thy burden far more light,
Than the bonds which bind us sadly
    In this world of sin and blight:
So we plunge through life's wild ocean,
    And, though loud its tempests roar,
With Thy cross, our brightest emblem,
    Struggle towards the eternal shore.

———

"UN SOUPIR VIENT SOUVENT D'UN SOUVENIR."

"Of remembrance oft there comes a sigh"
    When we think of the years so soon sped by,
Of days when the future we troubled not,
    And the past with its sorrows—soon forgot;
Of days when we revelled in pleasure's maze
    And feasted our being on words of praise,
When e'en the Most High was unheeded, till
    He bowed our proud hearts by His holy will.

A sigh of remembrance often comes
    When we think of our childhood's happy homes,
Where the star of affection brightly shone
    Now it has vanished—all, all are gone!

In yon churchyard see that fresh-made mound,
The grass is now growing green around,
And count ye the hopes now buried low—
They are spectral hopes of the "long ago."

Still, we thank the Lord in our morbid grief,
And know that our hearts He will give relief—
And we more fit for His home shall be
Where we hope to dwell for eternity.
So the sigh and remembrance grow more bright
When we think that the darkness shall turn to light;
And living in hope, we trust and pray,
That "the darkest hour is before the day."

CAUSES AND *EFFECTS*.

SOFT summer rain-drops, o'er the tired earth falling,
  Waking to life the fragrant, sweet spring-flowers,
Jewelling the green leaves all so brightly—
  Cooling the tender buds sweet summer showers !

So in my heart a *kindly* word hath rested,
  Causing the tears in thankful love to flow
Through a dark hour, and led my impulse higher,
  And taught my life a holier aim to know.

Deeply the tenderness, still o'er me sweeping,
  Brings back sweet thoughts, and makes me humbly pray,
That the *effect* may prove the *cause* held dearly,
  And that my heart those gentle words may sway.

Flow on, sweet showers!—and bid the buds to blossom
  Speak on, "kind words!"—thy accents ever dear
Shall lighten many a cloud through toilsome pathways,
  And many darksome moments brightly cheer.

8*

SHADOWS.

SADDER, sadder, grows the evening
  Of the life, too soon begun,
Grayer, darker falls the twilight
  On the task not yet half done,
While more sadly sinks the spirit
Neath the grief it doth inherit—
Bringing little fruit—less merit—
  All upbraiding—no hope—none.

Sadder—memory painteth ever
  Scenes that hold us captive still,
Whose soft shadows lengthen round us
  Slowly clambering up the hill.
Is there no bright beacon shining,
As the day's so fast declining?
Are there no fair flowers entwining,
  With sweet scents the air to fill?

Is this life all false, all shallow?
  Must these years of youth speed by,
Leaving *trackless* all the footpaths
  That should lead the soul so high?
Must our heart's best hopes be crushing
With these dreadful streams outrushing
All our cherished longings *hushing*—
  Must they all be born to die?

Calmly wait! all crosses grasping—
  Think! this life will soon be o'er,
And we'll find these heart-hopes flowering
  Where flowers bloom to die no more.
And a glorious day then shining,
Far beyond our best divining—
No more weeping, no repining,
  When we reach that peaceful shore.

PATIENCE.

Patience!—though thy life be dreary,
 And each day brings deeper pain,
Patience!—though thy heart be sinking
 Soon in joy 'twill beat again.
After every storm, the sunlight
 Glows more radiant than before —
There will be some quiet evening,
 When this long, long day is o'er.

Patience!—though thy cup be flowing
 With life's sorrows, bitter, deep,
Patience, like an angel watching,
 Soothes our restless hearts to sleep.
Patience!—see round dear old ruins
 Lovingly the ivy clings,
And to bind the broken casements,
 Brightest of its leaves it brings.

Patience, then—toil on, toil ever!—
 God above is righteous, true,
Let us live but for Him only,
 Strong and firm in all we do.
Strong to love and firm to conquer,
 When the Cross seems hard to bear
Let us ask our Blessed Mother
 In her gentle gift to share.

LINES WRITTEN ON WITNESSING A CEREMONY OF RELIGIOUS PROFESSION.

In a little convent chapel,
 In the dim, gray morning light,
Came unto all hearts a Presence,
 Mystic, radiant, living, bright!

Came unto three pure young spirits
  Loudly breathing vows of love;
Who, before that spotless altar,
  Chose their Spouse, the eternal Dove.

God of Mercy! these *Thy* chosen
  Heard Thy voice, obeyed Thy call:
For Thee leaving home and home-loves
  Giving Thee not *one*, but all;

For Thee broke the "captive fetters,"
  Severed every earth-bound tie;
Thinking of their future, promised,
  Cloudless home beyond the sky;

Offered Thee their hearts untarnished,
  Thou hast taken, made Thine own;
Shielded them from life's *fierce* tempest
  That they might love *Thee* alone.

All for Thee ! O loving Jesus !
  This *their* portion, oh, how sweet!
They are resting on Thy bosom,
  Help us, kneeling at Thy feet.

CLOUDS.

DARK shadows, sweeping o'er our life's horizon,
  Seem often to obscure all hope of day,
While sinking hearts await the dreaded climax,
  From which there shines no bright, inspiring ray.

And while these clouds are all our hopes o'erwhelming,
  We almost feel that God forgets we live,—
That God of mercy, love, untold compassion,
  Who seeth all, and will His blessing give.

Who seeth all! Oh, let us ask His pity
  To stay the sorrows gathering thick and fast;
Ask Him to make our proud hearts purer, gentler,
  And holier too, when the fierce storm has passed.

Ask Him to bless the Cross whereon He binds us,
  To bear with love, e'en tho' our hearts may break,
To live so that His blessed voice may call us,
  And bid us at His right our places take.

BELLS.

Toll! toll! toll!
    Toll in the joy of grief,
      Sacrifice, penance, prayer,
      Power the Cross to bear,
    Life is at best but brief—
              Toll! toll!

Toll! toll! toll!
    Bells, sounding sorrow-sweet,
      Echoes of love and praise,
      Heroic, heart-wrung lays,
    Sounds for God's service meet—
              Toll! toll!

Toll! toll! toll!
    Toll in the Advent days,
      Memories of by-gone years,
      Chequered with smiles and tears,
    Wondrous with God's dread ways—
              Toll! toll!

Toll! toll! toll!
    Humbled at Jesus' feet,
      Pale with the power of prayer,
      Strong with the will to bear,
    Toll sounds for victors meet—
               Toll! toll!

Toll! toll! toll!
    Toll out this wondrous year,
      Yet with a silvery sound,
      Till our sad hearts rebound,
    With hope exempt from fear—
               Toll! toll!

Toll! toll! toll!
    Toll through the coming time,
      Toll with a joy serene,
      Borne from the world unseen,
    Toll like a Christmas chime—
               Toll! toll!

Toll! toll! toll!
    Grace to this weary heart,
      Thoughts of how Jesus died
      Trampled on, crucified,
    Pierced with a traitor's dart—
               Toll! toll!

TO REV. FATHER CLOWRY.

When leaving to visit Ireland.

THY native home is circled
  By Atlantic waters bright,
And its sunlit hilltops glisten
  Neath the trembling rays of light.

Its sea-girt shore reposeth
   Under heaven's holiest smile,
Shedding peace, and hope, and comfort
   O'er Saint Patrick's chosen isle.

Do we wonder that thy footsteps,
   After years of life, should stray
Back where thy heart's first memories
   Rise, like a beacon's ray ?

Back, where thy boyhood's lesson
   Of deep, unerring truth
Fraught with honest faith and purpose,
   The aspirings of thy youth.

Do we wonder at the yearning
   Which thy manly heart yet fills,
Yearning to wander once again
   Among those verdant hills—

That the sparkling waters woo thee
   From life's sadder scenes away,
From the gloomy rays of evening
   To the dazzling light of day ?

No; a voice from home is calling
   With a merry, gladsome ring,
Waking in thy heart the echoes
   That life's early friendships bring.

Worthy friends have gathered round thee,
   Kindred spirits, true and dear,
But thy native home is dearer
   And thy native sky more clear

Than the brightest star that gleameth
   O'er our great, though foreign land.
For thee, Erin's dimmest beauty
   Bears an aspect far more grand,

Far more grand those ancient ruins,
　　Which in honored dust lie low,
Than all artist's skill can sculpture,
　　That no stranger heart can know.

How they breathe of saintly worship,
　　For their record is of saints,
Whose bright histories are shaded
　　By the pall that ruin paints.

And, when thine eyes are resting
　　Where ancestral homes have stood,
Where stone on stone is watered
　　By such bitter tears of blood,

Think that many of our sisters
　　Have left dearest heart-hopes there,
And with spirit raised to heaven,
　　Breathe for them a silent prayer.

May the angels guide thee, Father,
　　Not o'er life's calm waves alone,
But when time with mystic shadows
　　O'er thy heart its gloom has thrown,

Still the Sisters' prayers attend thee
　　O'er the trackless ocean's foam,
While, with grateful hearts, they wish thee
　　Safe in Ireland—safe at home.

———

REV. FATHER BURKE, O.P.

Voice of my country, son of ancient Erin,
　　Son of her soul, descendant of her heart,
Priest of the Lord in thy bright youth anointed,
　　And called and sent to preach "the better part."

O Father Burke! how hath thy word awakened
  The loving Irish past that long had slept,
And brought me home to Erin, to my country,
  And stirred my heart with joy, although I wept.

Joy, to hear once again the name of Erin,
  Spoken in love and praise, and yet hot tears—
Tears for her many sorrows, for the traces
  Of '48, that memory's bosom wears.
Blessed be God who sent us in our exile
  Thy voice of power to speak of faith and truth,
Of God and holy Church, and prayer, and penance,
  And all that Erin loves in age and youth!

Blessed be God, again her sacred ruins,
  Her holy Abbeys, and her Round Towers hoar
Are named exultingly, and their dear story
  Told like a Gospel to the world once more.
Her seven churches,—Clonmacnoise, Clondalkin,
  Cong and Armagh, and all her ruined fanes,—
Named to her children's hearts with such a power
  As makes them dearer for time's hoary stains.

Yes, blessed be God, again we've heard it spoken
  Proudly and lovingly, O'Connell's name,
Our own O'Connell, Ireland's Liberator,
  And heard it 'mid a people's loud acclaim.
O Father Burke! there is no way to thank thee,
  No words to tell of what our deep hearts feel;
Only an exile, hunted out of Erin,
  Can thus rejoice to hear thy proud appeal

To history and the past, and wring her glory
  Out of what men call shame, and make her known,
Fearless in faith and love and perseverance,
  Virgin and martyr, peerless and alone.

Son of St. Dominic, heir of his wide mantle,
  Oft shall thy name be mingled with our prayers;
Sisters of Mercy, servants of the suffering.
  We know the people's woes, and joys, and cares,

And bless the Lord who sent thee thus to cheer them
  To elevate their hearts, and make them stand
Steady beside the cross, sons of the martyrs,
  Steadfast in faith and love of fatherland;
Steadfast in love of Jesus and of Mary,
  True to the Holy Father as of yore;
Bound to the Church One, Holy, Apostolic,
  Roman and Catholic for evermore.

ON SPENDING AN EVENING IN "MARY'S ABBEY."

WHAT is it that we weep for most,
    As youth's bright days depart?
  Is it the glee so early lost
    Of a gay and careless heart?
  Or is it the blight of those brilliant schemes
    Whereon we loved to dwell!
  Or is it the wreck of our glad day-dreams
    That we weep for so wildly well?

  Or the gay air-castles with toilless art,
    Built all of hope and love,
  With garnishing from fancy's mart
    Of song and glory wove?
  Oh, these, alas! are passing away,
    Too soon their bright reign ends;
  Yet not for them do I weep to-day—
    I weep for my early friends.

Gone o'er the falsely smiling sea
On fame's wild path are some;
And in pleasant places far from me,
Have others made their home;
And I from the halls where we used to meet,
With a sad and an altered mien,
And shed hot tears o'er the memory sweet
Of the joys that of old have been.

A NUN.

To suffer—'tis to be a nun,
Wedded and vowed and bound,
While nature's fond affections yet
Thrill the young heart around.

But oh, such glorious suffering!
How blissfully the Bride
That Christ has called and sanctified,
Thus suffers at His side.

For He is near, His Sacred Heart
Supports her till she dies—
A holocaust of love divine,
A virgin truly wise.

Then shall the broken heart be healed,
The struggling spirit freed,
Eternal fruit of joy be reaped
From the dark, earth-sown seed.

SAINT JOSEPH !

DEAR, faithful guardian of the Infant Saviour,
Spouse and protector of our Mother mild,
Through the first dawns of sorrow, all-unearthly,
Gleaming around the Virgin and the Child.

May we, Saint Joseph, at thy shrine pay homage,
  May our poor words of praise to thee be sung,
We, who have strayed afar, foot-sore and weary—
  Who from His Infant-Heart such tears have wrung.

May we bow down in humble love, revering
  Thy fond heart's worship and unceasing care
Of Jesus and of Mary—through life's pathways
    May we to them, through thee, speed our poor
      prayer!

Holy Saint Joseph! by the desert wanderings
  Through night's dark shades into a land unknown,
By thy long dwelling 'mid an alien people
    Whose blindness scorned the light around them
      thrown.

Ah! by the sorrows that were thine with Mary's,
  Hear the poor heart that fain would speak to thee
In deep-abiding love, and trust, and homage,—
  Dearest Saint Joseph, hear in charity.

Be with us ever in this life's dread conflict,
  Comfort and aid, lest we should miss the goal
To which thy love can lead us, blest Saint Joseph—
  Oh, may that love our weary lives control.

Be with us, Father, when at last the summons
  Shall call us hence,—oh claim that hour thine own;
And let our spirit's flight, through thy dear pleading,
  Find *rest* beneath the footsteps of His throne.

Dearest Saint Joseph! Patron, Guide, Consoler,
  Of life's last moments and life's destiny!
Stand by us then, with Jesus and with Mary,
  And the " dark vale " all luminous shall be.

ON PARTING WITH SOME OF OUR SISTERS FOR A FOUNDATION.

THERE is no sorrow, Lord, but not to love Thee,
  There is no parting but to part from Thee,
There is no home but Thine, no hope but solely
  That which points to Thee o'er life's stormy sea!

Life hath no ills, if only we are faithful
  To that sweet grace, which sweetens them and fills
The heart with strength and courage, until sorrow
  Into a gladness strange and wondrous thrills!

Earth, our old mother-earth, so green and flowery,
  Loses its hold upon the hearts that fling
Their burden down before the feet of Jesus,
  And to His love and service ever cling!

But now a parting comes to try how truly
  Our hearts reëcho these exulting words;
How truly they have burst the ties that bound them,
  How unreservedly they are our Lord's!

"Rise my beloved and come!" again resoundeth
  Within the hearts we love so truly well;
And they are ready—to their Saviour's harvest
  They go with joy—yet sadly say farewell!

How shall your Sisters prove how much they wish you
  All blessings in your new and sacred home,
That after you, and with you, to our Saviour
  'Many with burning hearts of love may come!

Time shall go by, and round you shall be gathered
  Children to love Him daily more and more
Each passing day; yet will you oft remember
  St. Catherine's and the pleasant days of yore!

Will you not cling with more than mother's feeling
 To those who share your destiny, and leave
Their mother and their home once more for Heaven,
 Another victory for its sake achieve?

Alas, our own dear Sisters! shall we meet them
 No more while e'er life's changeful days shall last?
No more, no more—the very sound is sorrow,
 For it recalls the sorrow that is past!

Yes, we shall meet them in the bliss of Heaven,
 Meet them in glory and to " part no more;"
Meet them where death and sorrow cannot enter,
 Where tears and sighs and partings all are o'er!

Then there is no true parting, O my Saviour!
 But that which parts us from Thy peace and love;
For those we leave for Thee we shall find with Thee,
 If once we reach Thy glorious realms above!

—

THE SIGNAL STAR.

WHILE I gaze upon yon clear, bright star,
Its silvery light beams forth afar;
Recalling visions of days long past,
As the tide of time shall sweep all at last.
To those scenes shall memory oft turn with a sigh,
When my brow was cloudless as that blue sky;
And my heart was free, and my spirit light
As the balmy breath of a summer night;
When hope's gay dream was all as young
As the new-born note on some blithe bird's tongue:
But the rays of that star, bright tho' they be,
Shall fade in a moment, as hope from me.

Yet, oh! how well do I love to gaze
On thy pure, mild, and celestial rays;
And feel 'twould not unholy be
To offer a hymn of praise to thee!
But thou leadest my spirit higher far,
To Him who's enthroned above upper air—
Ah! why do mine eyes rest so long on thee,
And lingeringly dwell with ecstasy
On all thy loveliness shown in the night,
On thy far off lustre, so strangely bright?
She, my bosom's love since infancy's hour,
Whose faith is not even in fate's dread power;
Whom misfortune, not all her ills can change,
Nor destiny in her circling range,—
She—my sister—my friend—my all—to me
Sends forth her love all holy and free,
To mingle with mine in that pure sphere
Of all that is hallowed, and bright, and clear.
And thou art a sign, sweet star, to teach
The hearts, and minds, and spirits of each,
To dwell with the other in that dear hour
Of thine all-preserving power—
And though distance thus keepeth us far apart,
Bright star, thou'rt a sign in each Sister's heart!

SAINT COLUMBA'S FAREWELL.

STOOD Columba resting sadly
In the quiet summer sunset;
Resting from his farewell labors,
Long farewell to friends and neighbors:
Stood Columba, sun-rays gladly
Gilding each gray rock and runlet.

Saint Columba, in his tender,
Loving, fearless, Irish heart,—
He was praying, inly praying,
While the sunset's rays were playing,
For his people—their defender,
He, with faith and poet-art.

Aged was the Saint: beside him
True and faithful, Dermod stood;
Stood to help the aged Father,
While the tear-drops slowly gather:
Let no worldly heart deride him,
Mourning for the great and good.

Then Columba, looking seaward,
Blessed Iona, sea and strand;
Blessed the golden heaps of corn,
Blessed the kine, the sheep new-shorn;
Blessed the monastery, leeward,
Safe on its green nook of land.

Death was near, and St. Columba
Angel wings saw hovering near;
Earth was falling from his thinking,
As the sun was seaward sinking:
Heaven is coveting Columba's
Heart, whence love had cast out fear.

Then his old white horse drew near him, *
And his eyes were sad and dim;
Laid his head upon the shoulder,
Now grown old, alas! and older,—
Poor white horse there, standing near him,
Hearing not the angels' hymn.

---

* *See* " Monks of the West." Vol. III, page 264.

Turned be from the heavenward splendor,
Turned he to the horse so old;
Stroked his mane and bade them guard him,
And from cold and hardships ward him:
Dear Columba's heart so tender!
Wealth of love it left untold.

Helped by Dermod, then Columba
Sought the monastery's shrine;
Prayed that evermore his spirit
Erin's children might inherit:
In the twilight prayed Columba,
For his native land and mine.

Death was coming. Heaven was nearing,
Life was soaring up, away;
Saint Columba died in blessing.
Oh! the sorrow so distressing,—
As his last words they are hearing,—
Of his brethren who can say?

Died Columba ere the morning,
Died the Abbot great and true;
Died all purified and fervent,
Glorified as Christ's true servant:
Now Columba, earth-life scorning,
Sings the song for ever new.

ST. SEBASTIAN.

Bound and pierced, behold Sebastian,
  Firm and faithful to the last;
True to Jesus, though the arrows
  Fall around him thick and fast.

9

Though they pierce his flesh, and torture
    All his being into pain;
Love and sacrifice exalt him,
    While his blood is shed like rain.

Trial only perfects virtue,
    Suffering only deepens love;
Now Sebastian, God's dear martyr,
    Reigns in the bright heaven above.

Be as faithful now, dear sister:
    Be as true to Christ, your Spouse;
He who bought you with His life-blood:
    Made you His by veil and vows.

CONTRITION.

Jesus, Jesus, Jesus!
    Set my heart on fire;
Be Thou, sweetest Jesus,
    All my soul's desire!

Only let me love Thee,
    Then I ask no more;
Kneeling in Thy presence
    I my sins deplore!

True, too true, my Jesus,
    I've offended Thee;
Heart-wrung in my sorrow,
    From the world I flee!

Flee to thee, my Saviour,
    Take this sad, sad heart;
Take it, it is bleeding,
    Crushed in every part!

Thou hast made earth's pleasures
Bring me bitter pain;
My soul in anguish left them,
Ne'er to look again!

Often hast Thou called me:—
Years passed on; I came
To love and bless Thee, Jesus,
And to praise Thy name!

Sweetly hast Thou called me,
From Thy throne of love;
Breathing through my spirit
Joys of heaven above!

ON THE CONSECRATION OF IRELAND TO THE SACRED
HEART OF JESUS, PASSION SUNDAY. 1873.
[On which occasion Very Rev. T. N. BURKE, O.P., preached.]

Is the green Isle Thine, Lord Jesus?
Have they bound its people all,
In sweet bonds of love's devising
At Thy own all-potent call?
Have they knelt down in their sorrow,
And in faith and love and hope,
Consecrated all their manhood
For Thy sake with ill to cope?

Mothers, maidens, little children,
All are consecrated now;
May the Heart of Jesus bless them,
As they keep this glorious vow.
Oh I bless Thee, Jesus, Saviour,
Though from Erin far apart,
That I've lived to see my country,
Sacred to Thy Sacred Heart.

That our martyr mother-island,
　　Is found faithful as of old;
That in darkened days she clings to
　　Christ's dear Vicar, Christ's dear fold.
Holy Father, Pio Nono,
　　Ratify this act of love;
Lord, accept the vows of Erin,
　　In Thy glorious courts above.

And the exiles, dearest Jesus,
　　Are they consecrated too?
Did they think of them in Erin,
　　As they gave their lives to you?
Father Burke, dear friend of Erin—
　　Speaking of the Sacred Heart,
Did you pray that all her exiles
　　In that act might have their part?

———

TO A SISTER ON HER BIRTHDAY.

'Tis your birthday—may it ever
  Find you thus a child of grace;
Years will come—ah may they never
  Youth's sweet cheering hope efface!

Richened by the love of Jesus,
  Strengthened by the Bread of Life,
May my novice-child be always
  Victor in the spirit's strife.

May the Virgin Mother keep her
  Ever near to Jesus' feet,
Guide and guard, and help and bless her
  Till her triumph is complete.

Till she *vows* her love to Jesus,
  Till she prostrates as His bride,—
His in life, in death, in sorrow,
  Ne'er to part from His dear side.

PRAYER FOR A SISTER.

THREE graces, dearest Saint, obtain
  For this thy namesake child,
That her young heart may be, like thine,
  Holy and undefiled.

Self-sacrifice and love of God,
  Obedience to His will,—
These virtues, dearest Saint, I pray
  Into her mind instil.

Just three and twenty are her years,
  Like thine in this at least, —
Oh may her place resemble thine
  At Heaven's eternal feast.

To God, and "God alone," she gave
  Freely her bright young life—
For His dear sake, protect her in
  Temptation's weary strife.

FEAST OF SAINT AGNES.

WRITTEN FOR REV. MOTHER AGNES, IN 1855.

ONE glance at the dread arena, one thought of Imperial
    Rome,
And before the Christian's fancy, martyrs and heroes
    come:
Heroes of faith, who lifted the Cross to its place on high,
And in Christ, the Lord, exulting, went forth for His
    love to die.

Some from historic Asia, some from the Grecian isles,
From where the Arctic summer in sudden beauty smiles,
Maidens and youths and matrons, and old men worn and
    faint,
Have laid down their lives for Jesus, but none like this
    sweet young saint.

None like the Roman maiden, the flower of the Church's
    spring,
Whose death for her blessed Saviour, its choirs shall ever
    sing.
A child in her simple beauty, fragile and meek and fair,
In her white baptismal vesture, her flowing golden hair.

Dark is the Tullian prison, darker the hearts of men,
Yet the Virgin's face is wearing its rapturous look again;
Into the light of Heaven, beyond the Italian skies,
Gazeth the fearless maiden up with her love-lit eyes.

Bonds for the martyr, bring them, fetters of iron strong;
But the fetters of love are stronger, the Love she had
    worshipped long.
Chosen among a thousand—chosen for evermore—
Bride of the Lamb, He calls thee; soon shall the strife
    be o'er.

As a flower on the falling waters, borne by their fury on,
The saint, 'mid the Roman rabble, in the light of the
    Saviour shone.
She sees not the dread arena, she sees not the cohorts
    stand,
She sees not the gleaming arms, she sees not the blood-
    stained sand;

For a light from the inner Heaven streams on that fair
    young brow,
And the rapturous look is beaming, the girl is an angel now,
Already her sister-angels beckon her to their home,
Already she hears their anthems, and, joyous, exclaims
    "I come!"

Smiling, she shakes the fetters off from her tiny hands,
And gathers the golden ringlets, and calls to the quail-
    ing bands,
"A Christian to Christ devoted, espoused to the Lord
    alone,
Brothers, I bless the torture that sends me before His
    throne."

One stroke, and the fair form quivered, sinking at once
    to death,
While the glorified hosts of Heaven welcome her latest
    breath;
One stroke, and the white robe seemeth, like garments of
    Bosra, dyed,
And the soul of the virgin martyr with Mary is side
    by side.

Gone from that scene of horror, straight to the feet of
    Him,
The Lamb, before whose effulgence glory and light are
    dim.

Oh! hath not the Lord endowed thee, mother, with
    special grace,
That the Saviour, who called Saint Agnes, should call
    thee to share her place.

Called thee into His vineyard, and gave thee the grace to
    bring
A heart by the world untarnished, a life in its joyous
    spring;
Who chose thee to guide unto Him, in Mercy's path of
    Love,
Many with thee to journey unto the realms above.

The name of the Virgin Martyr, the name of the Virgin
    Queen,
Both, both are your own, dear mother, happy thy lot
    hath been;
Happy and still more happy, if but your children's
    prayers
Could win for you myriad blessings, shield you from
    pangs and cares.

Hear us then, sweet Saint Agnes, hear us entreat, once
    more,
Thy aid for our own dear mother, thy aid till her life is
    o'er;
Thine be the hand to lead her, then, to that Mother's feet,
Who won all the gifts that made her a Spouse for her
    Saviour meet.

ON THE DEATH OF SISTER MARY FRANCIS MAC K.

HARK! 'Tis a seraph's cry,
The holocaust is o'er,
A phœnix from its ashes rises
To die no more.
        A palm she bore.

ANGELIC CHOIR.

Hail, Sister, hail!
Thy work of love is done.
Come, join our blessed, happy band,
In this our ever lovely land—
        The crown is won.

SERAPH.

She comes, the consecrated one,
With the signet on her brow,
She bears the lily in her hand,
She cannot linger now.
        She has kept her vow.

ANGELIC CHOIR.

Hail, Sister, hail!
Thy work of love is o'er,
Go speed thee on thy glorious way,
To rest—to toil no more.
        The cross she bore.

SERAPH.

On, Sister, on,
Thy place is high above,
The King awaits thee on His throne,
Beyond the loftiest zone,
        With ardent love.

ANGELIC CHOIR.

Hail, Sister, hail!
   Thy joy has now begun,
Haste, join thee to the Virgin band,
The first in this our happy land.
    The victory is won.

On, on, she wings her joyous flight
   To highest heavens, through realms of light,
The Lamb's sweet canticle to sing,
   With her lily white and the signet ring
    Of her Spouse and King.

                M. C. S.

QUID RETRIBUAM?

WHY am I fastened to the earth
With spirit of immortal birth?
Rouse up, my soul, and look above,
Where sits enthroned the God of love.

Look up, look high, and let desire,
With eagle-eye and heart of fire,
Gaze upon Him thy soul holds dear,
Sweet, humble hope will banish fear.

Long for the place, the lowest, least,
Where for eternity thine eyes may feast
On Jesus, on Him Crucified,
Thy victim who was sacrificed.

To mark the glorious streams of light,
Emitting from the loving wounds
Of hands and feet and blessed side,
Where hope and joy and peace abide,

And the throbbings deep of His mighty Heart,
Where all His dear Redeemed have part—
Oh! will eternity be too long
To sing the Quid Retribuam,
    Et Deo nostri da Gloriam ?

M. C. S.

THE GARLAND.

I'VE woven a garland of flowers
  For thee, my little friend,
Where roses, lilies, and violets blue,
  Their sweetest fragrance blend,
Narcissus, Fuschia, all combine
Their beauty in this wreath of mine,
Wild berries, pansies, bright blue bell;
To thee in mystic language tell

A lesson, how the things of earth,
  So sweet and fresh and dear,
But bloom awhile and fade away,
  They have no dwelling here;
Their leaves will scatter in the blast,
  Must fade, and withered lie;
While the flowers of Heaven, mark it well,
  Will never, never die.

So let the Rose, divinest love,
  To thy gentle heart oft speak,
The pansies and the violets blue,
  Of a spirit mild and meek,
The blue bell and wild berries too,
  Sweet innocence will show,
While the lily in its purity
  In Heaven will ever blow.

M. C. S.

THE FLOWERS OF THE CROSS.

CHRISTIAN soul, in your visits to the Garden of the Cross,
Where you tread down earthly pleasures, their follies and
    their dross;
Have you marked the beauteous flowers which grow be-
    neath the shade
Of a Tree so good and fertile, by the Blood of Jesus made?

These flowers shed sweetest fragrance in the stable cold
    and bare,
Inhaling their best perfume from the Infant sigh breathed
    there,
From a Heart so full of mercy, of tenderness and love,
It burned to die for sinful Man, and left a throne above.

These followed in the traces by His bloody footsteps made,
Till 'neath the summit of the Cross they bloom within
    its shade;
These flowers hold in their little hearts a wondrous potent
    charm,
For all the countless ills of life there dwells a sovereign
    balm.

No cup of human sorrow, nor draught of bitterest woe,
These mingled in the potion, a sweetness thence must
    flow;
Then gather up a nosegay of things so sweet and rare,
And take them on your daily rounds of Blessed Mercy's
    care.

Go, place them on the sufferer's couch, where bending,
    cross in hand,
You kneel to pray for Peace and Love, they come at your
    command;
Or show them to the glazing eye, to fix its trembling ray,
Your flowers emit a cheering light to lumine Death's dark
    way.

To the bier where the desolate mourner weeps, your
    precious flow'rets bring,
And strew them o'er the darkened pall, they take from
    death its sting;
For Faith looks onward, far above this passing world of
    ours,
Hope pointing to the lov'd and lost, in Eden's blessed
    bowers.

In the gloomy cell, where vice and chains may form a
    living tomb,
Display your flowers, they dart a ray to chase the heaviest
    gloom;
Placed on the sinner's hardened heart, O! mark the
    crumbling rock,
The flinty stone His love hath reft, Who bled at Calvary's
    shock.

For the young and innocent of heart, where Purity must
    dwell,
O crown them with your precious flowers, for Jesus loved
    them well;
To these they are a pledge secure of happiness divine,
To you as stars in firmament, most glorious to shine.

Then prize your flowers, your deathless flowers of Faith
    and Hope and Love,
You tread a Godlike path below, it leads to Heaven above,
Where Faith and Hope, their mission o'er, all lost in blest
    reality,
Sweet Love with you its centre gains, the Bosom of the
    Deity.

                              M. C. S.

ST. JOSEPH'S PREACHER.

No one to do thee honor, dear St. Joseph,
    No one to preach on this thy festal day,
No one to stir our souls with love of Jesus,
    As only God's anointed can and may.
No one to tell how tenderly, how sweetly,
    Yet with what reverential awe the while,
You clasped the Infant Saviour to your bosom,
    And dried His tears and sought to make Him smile;

To tell how Mary, our sweet Virgin Mother,
    Depended upon you in every care,
How with most humble meekness she obeyed you,
    She knelt with you in humble, earnest prayer.
No one to move the people's hearts to love you,
    No one to preach on this most blessed theme,
Ah yes, dear Father Flynn from green old Erin
    Comes, bidden by the angels it might seem.

He came and told of Jesus and of Mary,
    Of Bethlehem and of the journey lone
Through the dread Desert into heathen Egypt,
    Touching all hearts with every word and tone.
Calling on Irish mothers to make Mary
    Their model and their patroness and friend,
Bidding them bring their children to the altar
    And make their being worthy of its end.

Calling on Irish maidens to be Irish
    In truth and modesty and virtue pure;
Bidding them be the honor of their people,
    And for the Faith all trials to endure.
Teaching them how to honor dear St. Joseph,
    How to be children of the Angel's Queen,
How to be faithful to the land that bore them,
    St. Patrick's Island, ever fair and green.

Farewell, dear Father, back to the Blackwater
  And Cappaquin with all their woodlands wild
You go rejoicing, yet to meet a sorrow,
  For he is gone who blessed you as his child.
"Soggarth aroon," when at dear Erin's altars
  You offer the great sacrifice, oh pray,
Pray for her exiled children, ask St. Joseph
  To guide them till they reach the realms of day.

SAINT PHILOMENE.

IN MEMORY OF OLD NOVITIATE DAYS.

St. Philomene—I've heard it said
  She knew but thirteen springs,
And yet that with the martyr-band
  The Virgin's song she sings.
Virgin and Martyr, life's young bloom,
  She laid at Jesus's feet;
A few short years, a glorious death,
  Her sacrifice complete.

Not thus your heavenward path is traced
  O'er life's arena-sand,
For up a long and steep ascent
  Its tortuous course was planned,
Now down 'mid valleys' umbrage hid
  And darkened into night;
Now over rock-built, arid piles,
  Half seen through gloomy light.

Now down upon the ocean's edge,
  Icy and wild and cold;
Now out among the lonely steppes,
  Where sheep can find no fold.
Now in the desert sunken deep,
  In hot, unhealthy sand;
Now on the sunlit hills, and now
  On the rich harvest-land.

On, on unshrinking, for aloft
  Shines Heaven's glorious light,
The Heaven Saint Philomene won
  In one short, fearless flight.
"Respice Cœlum"—martyrlike,
  Sister, pursue thy way,
Midnight and darkness, shade and gloom
  Pass, and behold! the day!

IN MEMORY OF THE CONSECRATION OF THE ARCHDIOCESE
OF NEW YORK TO THE SACRED HEART OF JESUS,
DECEMBER 8, 1873,

SACRED Heart of Jesus! Now we are Thine own,
Make us ever worthy of the graces thrown
O'er our lives in mercy on this blessed day;
Teach us to be faithful, lest our weak hearts stray
Ever from the fealty—sweetly vowed anew,
Through all cares and sorrows, Jesus! make us true!

Bless us, dearest Saviour! Bless our native shore,
Till its scattered children only Thee adore.
Bless the land, and love it, make it rich in grace,
May its freedom never Thy dear love efface.

Bless its broad, proud woodlands, fill its " homes and
        hearts "
With the grateful homage that Thy faith imparts.
May our own dear country, " noble, grand, and free,"
Break and bend its freedom only, Lord, for Thee.]
Guide her sons, Lord Jesus, near and far away,
Let their own hearts whisper, how this blessed day
From our beauteous Mother, Patroness, and Queen,
These poor hearts, unworthy, cold, as they have been,
Once again Thou takest to Thy Love Divine,
Once again Thou makest truly, wholly Thine;
Never to desert Thee, ne'er to cease Thy praise,
In all hours of peril on Thy Heart to gaze.
Sacred Heart of Jesus! Hear this feeble voice
Let its accents tell Thee how our souls rejoice,
That we are Thy children, that Columbus' land
Feels the tender pressure of Thy loving hand.
Consecrate it, Jesus! all, from shore to shore,
Love and guard and bless it, Jesus, we implore.
Mary—gentlest Mother—lead us to Thy Son,
Shield us 'neath thy mantle till the crown is won.

PART SECOND.

POEMS AND PLAYS

INTENDED

FOR CHILDREN ONLY.

POEMS AND PLAYS

INTENDED

FOR CHILDREN ONLY.

TO THE CHILDREN OF THE RICH FOR THE CHILDREN OF THE POOR.

DEAR little friends, whose eyes bespeak the gladness,
    That in your hearts like God's bright sunshine dwells;
Whose lives are filled with rays of home-affection,
    Twining o'er all such blissful, fairy spells.

List ye, and know, that hearts like yours are flowing
    With bitter sorrow,—and that bare, cold feet
Travel the city's walks, while ye are sleeping,—
    Seeking for warmth and shelter, in the street.

That little childish heads are bowed in anguish,
    That tiny fingers toil and know not play;
That crouching figures fear their home's reception,
    And shrink e'en from that sweet word, "home," away.

To them it echoes not in love,—they know not
    The cherished tenderness with which you hail
Each eve's unbroken circle,—joys and pleasures,—
    No ! they but see life's weary, darksome veil.

No gentle mother's smile to crown their labor—
    Perchance her soul hath winged its flight above ;
Or if remaining,—'tis the earth's cold bosom
    That speaks to her of future peace and love.

Sadly she folds her dear and suffering children
  Unto her heart, that would their comfort be;
But it is broken, and its songs are silent:
  Sorrow is very sad in infancy.

So, for the love of Jesus in His childhood,
  If to His Infant-Heart you would be dear,—
Cherish and keep the legacy He leaves you:
  His own afflicted little ones to cheer.

Think of your happy homes,—deal out a portion
  Of kindly comfort to your sadder friends;
Believe their prayers will reach the Heart of Jesus,
  Deepening the love, which on you now He spends.

FOR THE MONTH OF MAY.

CHILDREN, 'tis the month of Mary,
    Strew her altar-steps with flowers,
And your guileless witness bear
    What a genial faith is ours!
To our Blessed Lady offer
    Joyous hymns of love and praise;
Make atonement for the scoffer,
    For he knows not what he says.
May for you is doubly blooming,
    Life itself is in its Spring,
No dark clouds are o'er you looming,
    All seems fair and promising.

Therefore, to most holy Mary
    Consecrate your hearts and lives,
She will not forget her servants
    When their trial-hour arrives.

Wait then for no more to-morrows,
 Cast yourselves before her feet,
She will soften all your sorrows;
 She who is with grace replete,
In affliction will not leave you,
 But, when life has passed away,
Will with open arms receive you
 Into everlasting May.

In this blessed month of Mary
 Heavenly Father, grant to me
True devotion to that Mother
 Who alone was worthy thee;
Grief for every thing that grieved her,
 Joy for all that gave her joy;
And in those who've not believed her
 Worthy of our love, destroy
Whatso'er it is that blinds them,
 Through her suffering Son, we pray
Till at length Thy mercy find them,
 And they, too, to Mary pray.

HYMN TO THE BLESSED VIRGIN.

AIR.—"Mary, Mary, Queen of my Soul."

QUEEN of my soul, to whom are known
 My life, my hopes, my heart,
Behold me on thy mercy thrown,
 Who Queen of Mercy art.
Oh thou who canst all grief console,
Queen of my soul! Queen of my soul!
Mary! Mary! Queen of my soul,
Mary! Mary! Queen of my soul.

Mary, forget not I am one
   Of those poor souls who were
Bought by the life-blood of thy Son,
   Confided to thy care.
Oh, place me on thy client roll—
Queen of my soul! Queen of my soul!
               Mary! Mary! etc.

Queen of my soul! whose name imparts
   A sweetness none can tell
Unto thy loving children's hearts, —
   Oh, may it ever dwell
In mine, and all its powers control—
Queen of my soul! Queen of my Soul!
               Mary! Mary! etc.

Queen of my soul, may thy pure eyes
   Watch o'er me when I die,
And, as my trembling spirit flies,
   Be thou to guard it nigh,
And bear it to a blissful goal—
Queen of my soul! Queen of my soul!
               Mary! Mary! etc.

SAINT PATRICK'S DAY.

HOLY Patrick, patron blest
Of the land I love the best,
Once thy day brought joy and gladness,
Chasing far each thought of sadness,
When we sped at early morning,
Ditch, and hedge, and damp feet scorning,
To seek out some sheltered nook
Where the shamrocks greenest look,

Then sped home prepared for Mass,
Fixing high the triple grass
In boy's cap or young girl's bonnet
Where all eyes must rest upon it.
Sad the day I left my childhood,
As the time when some fair wild-wood
Where a myriad flowers bloom brightly,
And young fawns are bounding lightly,
Where rich berries hang in clusters,
And wild birds hold merry musters,
Is *cut down* and cleaned for tilling,
At some stern, old owner's willing.
Home is but a memory
Now, alas, to mine and me—
But from thee we've learned to know
That our home is not below:
Thou wert exiled, why not we ?
Oh were we but like to thee !
Dear St. Patrick, won't you pray
For those scattered far away,—
From the Isle whose very air
Breathes of God, of faith, of prayer,
Where, as in a record vast
We may read the hallowed past ?
Wreck and ruin and decay
Cannot blot that scroll away.

FOR A LITTLE IRISH EXILE.

ELLIE AROON, you want me to write for you "a piece,"
For you, my mother's grandchild, my namesake, and my
    niece,
Shall it be about the Fairies, in their robes of green and
    gold,
Who nightly 'mong the flowers their merry revels hold;

10

Who steal the milk and butter on the pleasant first of
        May,
If the farmer or his household one word against them
        say ?
Shall it be about the Giants and their dreadful Fee,
        Faw, Fum ?
Shall it be about Red Riding Hood or Jack or old Tom
        Thumb ?
Shall I tell you of Aladdin or the tale of Mother Goose,
Of Shelah and of Dermot who got such sad abuse ?
I know the dismal story of the Children in the Wood,
And rhymes, that sounded well of old, about bold Robin
        Hood ;
I could tell you of the Wishing Cap, and all about the Ball
Where Cinderella's slipper from her little foot did fall.
But, Ellie! you are Irish, and methinks I hear you say,
Tell me of Ancient Erin, of our old home far away ;
But the tale is long, dear Ellie! the tale is long and sad,
For centuries of sorrow, scant peace hath Erin had.
The Danes of old harassed her till gallant Brian Boru,
He made himself the monarch of the island through and
        through.
And from Clontarf he swept them, these Danes, into the
        sea,
Upon that blest Good-Friday and made his country free.
Our land had been the Isle of Saints, but these accursed
        Danes
Had rifled sacred temples and burned its holy fanes,
Had sacked her schools, and scarcely had the land found
        time to rise
When the Norman Strongbow lifted his banner 'neath
        her skies.
A crew of greedy rovers, a wild, adventurous race,
Half soldiers and half settlers. Christians in name not
        grace, —

These came, and then the Saxons, a mean, gold-seeking
    tribe,
And the Welshmen with Cambrensis, a false, foul-hearted
    scribe.
Soon England's king came over, Plantagenet the proud,
The second Henry, he whose fame in the Holy wars was
    loud.
Oh, then a weary strife began, and false McMorrough gave
His daughter and his kingdom both, to Stronghow, bad
    but brave.
Ah! then did coward hearts betray their native land and
    pay
Their homage at the stranger's feet who spurned them as
    they lay.
Ah vainly, vainly, Ellie, I try to tell you how how
Our country hath been furrowed by sorrow's ruthless
    plough.
But I must tell of Ulster's brave chiefs, the true O'Neils,
O'Donnells and McMahons, McKennas and O'Sheils;
These often made the strangers lament their deadly
    blows,
And stood between Old Ulster and her relentless foes:
In Munster, the McCarthys and O'Connors kept the field,
The O'Briens and O'Sullivans were never taught to yield;
There many a hard fought battle, and many a headlong
    flight
Of Saxons left to Erin once more her own birthright.
Poor Leinster suffered soonest, though Art McMurrough
    brought
His utmost might to aid her, as Art McMurrough ought ;
And the brave O'Byrnes defended the hills of Wicklow
    well,
As Essex at the Pass of Plumes with lowered crest could
    tell.

But Connaught, Celtic Connaught, it held out to the last,
The McDermotts and O'Connors kept their ancient
    strongholds fast:
It was there the craven English upon Galway's gates
    wrote thus,
"From the fierce and free O'Flahertys, O Lord, deliver
    us!"
But England grew in power, by fraud and force and
    guile,
She triumphed o'er the nations and o'er our native Isle.
Her rule has been a rule of blood, and hate and grief and
    crime,
For which the Lord will smite her, when comes his own
    good time;
She long ago betrayed the faith that St. Augustine taught,
And gold she made her God, and gold by treachery she
    sought.
Now let her god preserve her, now let his might prevail,
As from dread Balaklava her smothered groans we hail;
Now let her trade and commerce, her "wooden walls"
    defend
The guilty land, whose countless crimes the Lord has
    said must end.
Ah, in her wreck and ruin creation shall rejoice,
And thou, my own, my country, lift up at last thy voice;
Lift up thy voice, green Erin, sing, sing on all thy hills,
Is that thy harp's wild music my longing ear that fills?
Oh! I shall never see thee, but I could die in peace
If only o'er the ocean came the news of thy release!
Oh I shall never see thee, my dust shall never lie,
With my father's, in thy bosom, but for thee I could
    die!
Oh! I shall never see thee, but I will live for thee,
And for thy children labor, mavourneen, gra machree.

TO MARY ANNE ELIZABETH.*

MARY! whose power in heaven is such,
    That thou canst all things gain,
Keep this young heart from sin's foul touch,
    Bind it with love's sweet chain.
Love, strong as death for God and thee,
    Unto her soul impart,
And keep her true to it till she
    Shall see thee as thou art.

Mary! since thou hast favor found
    With God for sinful man,
Teach her the mighty depth to sound,
    As far as creature can,
Of thy Son's love, who died for her,
    And who for her remains
As if deprived of power to stir,
    Within our holy fanes.

Oh make her grow in grace and sense,
    And, as her years advance,
Let not the world, with false pretence,
    Its charms for her enhance.
Her names to thee were household words
    When thou on earth didst dwell—
Oh if her life with them accords,
    No tongue her bliss may tell.

Mary! thy holy name she bears—
    Let this her passport be,
Whene'er for comfort, in her tears,
    And help she comes to thee.

---

* The child to whom these lines were addressed, entered a convent before she was 17, and died a holy death at 21. She was called in religion Sister Mary Agnes.

Thy mother's name is also hers,
    And gives her a new claim
Upon thy heart which ever stirs
    To hear thy mother's name.

As thou didst haste to Hebron
    Thy cousin to attend,
So be thy mercy ever shown,
    So hasten to befriend
In every strait this little one,
    Who after her is named,
The mother of the great St. John,
    Whose gentle voice proclaimed

That thou wert full of every grace,
    The mother of the Word,
The mediatrix of our race,
    Well pleasing to the Lord.
And as thy coming to that house
    The Baptist sanctified,
By thy aid, may her holy vows
    Be kept, however tried.

Preserve the white robe stainless,
    Bestowed upon her then,
Her spirit pure and chainless,
    Until from earth again
She's summoned to partake in
    The marriage feast prepared
For those who, all unshaken,
    In the good fight have shared.

O Virgin Mother! hear me
    For this, my sister's child,
And keep her ever near thee,
    Although on earth exiled.

Sweet Mary! grief's Consoler!
Thy mantle o'er her cast;
When thou seest ill before her,
Screen her, till it be past.

If in her heart the leaven
Of sin should try to work,
Whisper to her of heaven,
Point where the demons lurk.
The grandchild of my mother,
Her namesake too she is,
For her sake, if no other,
Oh hear my prayer in this!

And, Mary Anne! while ever
Upon this earth you are,
Do not from Mary sever,
Look always to this star.
Learn from her blest example
The Lord your God to serve,
Whose goodness ever ample,
Does all your love deserve.

TO ELLEN MARY CLARE.

Oh Virgin ever holy, this little child behold,
Her soul, I pray thee lowly, unto thy heart enfold;
Tho' young, she has known sorrow—most clement Virgin!
     cheer,
Nor let it too much harrow one to thy servants dear.
Cheer her, thou Star of Morning! for her be Heaven's
     gate,
Behold thy name adorning her soul, nor let her wait
Vainly for thee, whose power, and mercy are alike,
But in temptation's hour deign in her cause to strike.

Mary! with whom the treasure of Heaven itself is stored,
By thee in plenteous measure for her be it outpoured;
Teach her to love with fervor thy well-beloved Son,
For thy sake He'll preserve her: for thou didst never shun
One drop of sorrow's chalice, but lovingly didst share
In all that our malice did for our Lord prepare;
In her heart let no rancor or pride of life find place—
Be thou her firm anchor, Glory of Eva's race!

Sweet Mother! make her worthy the Green Isle of her
    birth,
Where we all learned to love thee, thou purest child of
    earth;
Bless thou our country, Mary! her children to thee cling,
Oh let them not grow weary with their long battling;
Aid them 'gainst the stranger and his still stranger creed,
Through every scene of danger keep vigorous the seed
Thy servant, Pope Celestine, sowed by St. Patrick's
    hand,
And banish strife intestine, the ruin of our land.

And, Ellie dear, be ever true to the dictates high
Of the old land, though never, alas! may you or I
Gaze on her storied beauty—oh may you still pursue
The sacred path of duty she hath marked out for you—
Be a true child of Mary, and love her above all,
Let not that love e'er vary, whatever may befall;
Yes, love her above all things, except the Lord alone,
For love of Mary ever brings us nearer to His Throne.

The holy Cross of Calvary from which the Sacrifice
That makes our altars ever rich did to the Father rise,—
Religion's glorious centre, devotion's heart and soul,—
May faith in it increase each day, and spread from pole to
    pole.

St. Ellen found, with trouble and long and anxious care,
That Cross—do you redouble the fervor of your prayer,
That, as the mighty giver of all good gifts to thee
Has chosen to deliver this royal legacy,

You may with love embrace it, cling to it to the last,
By no rash act disgrace it, or ever try to cast
The weight from off thy shoulders which our loved Lord
     has borne,
Until thy body moulders in its sepulchral urn.
All in this world must bear it, whether for good or ill,
Thrice blest are those who share it with ready heart and
     will,
For it the Saints have gladly left all that they held dear—
Being thus of self bereft, their way to Heaven was clear.

That young and fragile maiden, of whom it made "St.
     Clare,"
Thought it the priceless pearl to which naught can com-
     pare;
Leaving her home, where every heart to hers had fondly
     clung,
She did not think too hard a lot for one so blest and
     young;
And God, who ever blesses the souls that to him turn,
Heedless the world's caresses as of its scoffs and scorn,
Bestowed on her the treasure for which alone she sighed,—
His love which brings a pleasure to all things else denied.
Mother of grace and mercy! again on thee I call,
Though I be all unworthy, oh let no ill befall,
No passion ever master this little niece of mine.
Till all thy own thou hast her, in blessedness divine.

THE GEOGRAPHY OF IRELAND.

WRITTEN FOR IRISH CHILDREN IN EXILE.

My native home is Erin, my own, my Father's land,
I love its flowery valleys, I love its memories grand;
The wild Atlantic ocean between us pours its tide,
Yet will I try to know it from North to Shannon side.

The North, green, fertile Ulster—I love it well, for there
The green, soft grassy hills are set, its ramparts strong
     and fair;
There Monaghan and Armagh stand, Cavan and green
     Tyrone,
And Donegal and Derry, where James was overthrown.

Fermanagh there its lakes of blue spread to the sun's
     bright rays,
And Antrim where the Causeway stands, where shines the
     broad Lough Neagh;
The Bann and the Blackwater, and the Foyle's broad
     sweeping flood,
And a thousand springs are pouring free thro' valley, plain
     and wood.

Leinster has twelve broad counties where Dublin city
     stands,
Liffey and Boyne, and Barrow flow through its fertile lands;
Wicklow, Kilkenny, Wexford, Dublin, Louth and Meath,
Kildare and Carlow, may they all the sword of discord
     sheathe.

Longford—the ancient Annaly's, a hospitable soil,
Though woefully her son's are pressed by tyranny and toil;
The ruins of her abbeys by the Crumlin's banks are seen,
And the name of Temple-Michael tells where a church
     hath been.

Alas, for Leix and Offaly! they bear an English name;
King's County and the Queen's they're called,—words
    redolent of shame;
And now I pass from Leinster and the ancient English
    pale,
Where Strongbow ravaged and where lived the famous
    Granu Aile.

Old Connaught! O my country, how all the bygone days
Saw heroes fill its homestead, and harpers hymn its praise;
Leitrim, Roscommon, Sligo, and Galway's famous town,
And Mayo with its Abbeys and Aughrim's sad renown.

Five counties, many a battle field, and many a holy shrine,
And many a tale of stormy strife, old Connaught, all are
    thine—
Southward is fertile Munster with its old Milesian fame,
And its learning, wild and racy, and its soul of restless
    flame.

The Shannon sweeps through Limerick and Tipperary
    bounds,
And Kerry where O'Connell's voice still in our thought
    resounds ;
Cork! the green island's borders contain no land more
    fair,
And near it Waterford is found, and westward ancient
    Clare.

Through Munster flows the pleasant Lee, and the sunny
    Avonmore,
And thy famous Lakes, Killarney, with all their fairy lore;
There Mangerton uplifts his brow, and Turk with all his
    woods
Of flowery arbutus, keeps guard around thy floods.

Thus thro' old Erin roving in sad and wistful thought,
My native land, my mother, may I love thee as I ought;
Thus early, early exiled, may still my heart be true,
O Martyr of the Nations! through good and ill to you !

To you I owe my faith, to you my hope in God on high—
Oh may His love still lead me on, till in that faith I die;
And may your long, dark sorrows cease, oh may we one
      day see
The Emerald Isle, the Ocean's gem, a happy land and
      free.

———

CHRISTMAS AND THE CHILDREN.

OLD Christmas is coming, his coat is white
      With its weight of crystalline snow,
And around his aged and hoary head
      The breath of the frost-winds blow.
But a merry face and a kind has he
      That tells of a happy heart,
Though he puts us in mind of the dear old times,
      Till the tears in our sad eyes start.

All holy thoughts and designs has he,
      All teachings most pure and high,
For he tells a tale of the Saviour's love,
      And of regions beyond the sky.
He takes the child by the fair young hand,
      And he leads to the stable cold,
And he points to the Virgin Mother there,
      To the Babe that her arms enfold.

He tells us the Gospel tale again,
      He shows us the path of life,
He warns us, with kindly and thoughtful love,
      Of the snares with which earth is rife.

He loves us all, and he sets apart
    For the children a welcome store
Of hopes, and presents, and pleasant things,
    And of merry and laughing lore.

To the school he comes, and his welcome shines
    On the youthful faces there,
And a murmur of gladsome hopes is heard,
    For each one expects a share.
For old Christmas has whispered in words of love,
    For our Pastor, and told him that we
Had all prepared for this busy day,
    And were longing his face to see.

And he comes as he often did before
    To aid us, and cheer and bless
The efforts we make in the upward way
    Which our struggling footsteps press.
And we pray that the happy Christmas-time
    May often return to him,
That blessings may gather round him, till
    Life's lamp burns low and dim.

———

WRITTEN FOR THE CHILDREN OF ST. JOSEPH'S INDUSTRIAL HOME.

FEAST OF THE EPIPHANY, 1871.

Not gold, nor precious stones,
    Nor costly gifts we bring,
But in a simple, little verse
    Thy name, sweet Babe, we sing.

Lured by the self-same glorious star
   That led the monarchs old,
In wondering love and ecstasy
   Their Saviour to behold.

We are but children, dearest Lord,
   And to Thy crib we come
To ask Thy loving heart to bless
   Our dear "St. Joseph's home."

This is our gala-day—our feast,
   Our dearest friends are here;
Tho' many loving smiles we miss
   That greeted us last year.

Ah! dearest Lord, *we* cannot thank
   Thy tender, gentle care,
But ask our kindly angel-guides
   To Thee our hearts to bear—

And through Thy Mother's love we ask
   Thy grace, that we may be
Ever her children good and pure,
   Till we go home to Thee.

THE GEOGRAPHER'S SCRUTINY.
(Written in 1860.)

OPENING SPEECH.

I'M Geographer general, come to inspect
The condition of things and all errors detect,
The "Orbis terrarum" (*terrorum*, in fact,)
Ought to keep in its orbit, precise and exact.
But there's such a commotion within and without,
That I fear it will knock all the planets about,
So, as it would seem that the "time's out of joint,"
I think an inspection is quite to the point.

And I call all the Countries—I see they are here—
To give an account of themselves without fear.
There's Asia, my beautiful, bountiful child,
With all sorts of climate from fierce down to mild,
With the wealth of Golconda, the treasures of Ind,
And beauty earth-strewn from Siberia to Scinde.
There she's lying asleep in the lap of the world,
The Mother of nations, her every flag furled—
I would rather a little disorder and spunk,
Than this "statu quo" state, into which she has sunk.

ASIA DEFENDS HERSELF.

Good Mr. Geographer, let me explain
(Though you seem to suppose I've a softening of brain),
Tho' I'm Asia, I'll act like an Irishman here,
And answer by asking a question:—'Tis clear
That I'm free to inquire by what sort of a right
You complain that I sleep and am not given to fight.
Your place is to question of rivers and bays,
Of mountains and valleys, of quagmires and quays,
Of deserts, oases, of lakes, and of seas,
And they're all at their posts as composed as you please.
There's China, Mongolia, the wild Tartar land,
The desert of Cobi, the Himalays grand;
The dashing Euphrates, "the calm Bendemeer,"
The Indus with waters so blue and so clear;
And Syria, the beautiful, rose-loving land,
Judea, where Mercy's dear monuments stand;
Where Calvary preaches and Thabor inspires,
And Sion seems thrilling us still with its lyres,
Where Carmel is fragrant and Hermon is fair,
And the Jordan is cooling the sweet evening air.
Ah, Mr. Geographer, here at my heart
Mankind had their birth—and the dullest wits start

Into deeper existence, more earnest, more true,
When the Asia of Scripture is brought into view.
But excuse me, I'm leaving my province, like you—
There's Europe—she'll find you out something to do.

GEOGRAPHER.

Yes, Europe,—I settled her up long ago,
And named every river from Danube to Po;
From frozen Spitzbergen to Cape Finisterre,
The land is laid out like a fine lady's hair:
So, Europe, come forward, you surely should be
The model division by land and by sea.

EUROPE REPLIES.

I should, I admit it—yet I must complain
That I find it quite hard all my states to restrain.
The poor Bay of Biscay is tired to death
Keeping France from extending out seawards for breath;
And the Pyrenees try to grow higher and higher,
To keep her from setting all Spain upon fire:
Spain herself keeps the Mediterranean in fears,
With her efforts to rush upon Fez and Algiers;
The Apennines ache with their onerous task,
To keep Italy still in the sunlight to bask,
For the whole Adriatic can't cool the hot air
That is killing the life in her provinces fair.
I see with regret every boundary line
That used to be sacred, now sadly repine—
Why even the islands hemmed in by the sea
Seem determined to act as if utterly free.
So don't be surprised to see Cyprus or Rhodes,
Or Malta or Mytelene change their abodes,
Since the *boss* of the islands, old England, has tried
For hundreds of years o'er the ocean to stride.
So, Mr. Geographer, hold yourself ready
To re-adjust me, tho' you thought me so steady.

GEOGRAPHER.

I'm really provoked—what can I expect
From poor Africa there, if my work is thus wrecked;
If Europe is wheeling about like "Jim Crow,"
Can we wonder if *Egypt is* found on tiptoe?

AFRICA.

'Tis too hot over there to be jumping about,
We're as dull as the strand when the tide is gone out:
The Pyramids stand as they always have stood,
And the Nile treats us still to its annual flood;
The Sahara is there just as sandy as ever,
And the sun turns his back on it never, oh never!
Here Congo and Zanguebar look to the seas
From opposite coasts in the hope of a breeze,
And old Ethiopia shut up in the centre—
As well might you into a hot oven enter.
Yet the tall camelopards and bounding gazelles
Find out the green oasis, the fresh-flowing wells,
Where, out in the solitudes, sandy and lone,
A mantle of verdure is over them thrown.
I pity myself—I'm a sinner, I know,
I'm burnt up all the time, tho' the tears often flow;
I'm awkward and dark, and my people are queer,
Unlike any other of whom I can hear;
My Kings are queer fellows, with feathers and rings,
And my Beys and my Deys do a thousand queer things.
That old Abder-Aman shut up in Algiers,
Brought the French and their cannon to bother my ears.
So though lazy by nature, they won't let me rest,
But gnaw like a vulture my sun-stricken breast;
Aye, Frenchmen and Dutchmen and fat Englishmen,
If I sleep for a minute, they rouse me again:
So, Mr. Geographer, do not perplex me,
If you ask any questions, you really will vex me.

America seems to be ready to face you,
Don't provoke her young blood, or you'll find that she'll
    chase you.

GEOGRAPHER.

Well, well, I'll be lenient and let you alone—
(I can't work much myself in that great torrid zone,)
The Nile and the Niger may go their own way,
Darfur and Loango do just as they may;
I'll turn to America, fearless and wild—
My youngest, my fairest, my favorite child.
Come forward, my darling, and tell us how fast
You diffused your hot life, through those solitudes vast:
How you planted the wilderness, gave it a name,
Made *States* out of prairies, *States* dear now to fame:
From Davis's Straits, down to Florida's end,
You're my most energetic disciple and friend.

AMERICA.

I'm almost overpowered with the praise I so love,
And for which with such terrible vigor I strove,
But to tell you the truth I have views of my own,
If they are not by inward convulsions o'enthrown:
You know I have splendid material at hand,
My rivers are glorious, my mountains are grand;
My bays and my harbors the finest on earth,
My provinces fertile have never known dearth;
I've the wealth of the mines, of the sea, of the soil,
And a *head* to direct it, and *sinews* to toil.
The mightiest oceans my boundaries are,
And quarrelsome continents keep away far.
So, Mr. Geographer, nature for me
Has done more than you can with your spectacles see.
Of that I won't boast—it would be but absurd—
But of my *political* exploits, a word:

By these I have made a wild continent tame,
Planted cities and states, and won fortune and fame,
Got up a Republic *unmatched* in the world:
May its Stripes and its Stars never *basely* be furled.
May it flourish for ever in union and peace,
May discord and rancor within its fold cease;
Like the silv'ry Pacific, calm, powerful, free,
May its thirty-four states for a thousand years be;
Like the stormy Atlantic, encounter their foes,
Whether traitors betray them, or nations oppose;
I'm *ready* for either: I'm strong, and I'm proud,
And youthful and ardent, and eager, and loud,—
Tho' perhaps when I've lived for some centuries more,
Like others, I'll seem travel-soiled and footsore.

GEOGRAPHER

Alas, too much *spunk* is as bad as too little!
Too much *steam* very often has "burst up" the "kittle;"
"Look to home," my dear friend, mind your treasures so
    rare,
I say to you solemnly, sadly, *beware!*
Oceanica, what can you say for yourself?
Tho' youngest of all, are you laid on the shelf?
Not a word do you say about all your sweet isles,
Where beauty perennially blossoms and smiles;
Won't you tell us your tale—won't you say in good truth,
That you're happy and blest in your innocent youth?

OCEANICA.

I have little to boast of—you know it of old,
I'm quiet and silent—not given to scold;
I live in a world of my own, far away
From the strife and the turmoil you heard of to-day.
The loveliest islands, the sunniest seas,
The sweetest of climates, the balmiest breeze;

Fruits matchlessly beautiful, flowers most fair—
All these are to me as familiar as air.
I have little to do with the rest of my race,
And that little of sorrow left many a trace.
Secluded by nature, here mankind might be
From evil, and evil's fell consequence free;
Might make a new Eden, might sing a new song,
Which even the angels would catch and prolong;
Might make each fair island a beautiful shrine,
And faith like a garland around it entwine—
But I tire your patience. Good-bye till next year,
When I'll make my account more precise and more clear.

GEOGRAPHER.

I hope so indeed. May the years as they land,
One by one on your beautiful coral-strewn strand,
Bring you helps to develop the treasures you hide
In those regions long known but to ocean and tide;
May they bring you the faith and the love of our Lord,
And leave you with treasure of virtue well stored.
A word to America, strong in her youth:
Be a friend and an ally to genius and truth;
Let honor and conscience reign paramount through
The Union of States, and inhabitants too;
Be *Union* your watchword and soon they shall cease,
These rumors of discord, and sink into peace.
As for Europe and Asia and Africa there,
They 'll have their own way—so I leave them to share
The exuberant life of the glorious young West,
And for its improvement shall labor with zest.

A CHRISTMAS PLAY.

SPEECH OF CURIOSITY.

WHAT a fuss and a racket! what laughing, what glee!
Will nobody tell what the matter can be ?
Here's merry young faces, and funny young eyes,
And joyous young hearts too, that need no disguise.
But what are they looking for ?   Who is to come—
Will any one tell me ?   I'm sure you're not dumb.
Expectation on tip-toe is standing erect,
And what she expects I do want to detect.
For my name's Curiosity: never can I
See a fuss going on without knowing the why,—
So excuse me, if seeing you all so delighted,
My spirit essential becoming excited,
It bursts all the bonds of decorum so prim,
And compels me to beg you will humor its whim:
And tell me who's coming, what's all this about,
Who's hid by that curtain?   What means that gay shout ?

Curtain rises and SANTA CLAUS *comes forth.*

SPEECH OF EXPECTATION.

He's come!   It's himself!   It is old Santa Claus!
He's coming to keep up his own Christmas laws!
I expect he has every thing that can be made,—
From a chain of bright gold to a red candy spade:
His bag is far bigger than that of last year—
Dear me! how I wish he would come over here!
For I know all his pockets are stuffed with nice things,
Nice books and nice pictures, nice bracelets and rings.
I expect——But, dear me! I'm almost out of breath,
If he waits any longer I'll worry to death.

EXPECTATION *sits down quite exhausted, and* FUN *comes
out, looking of course quite funny.*

SPEECH OF FUN.

I'm prime minister here, or at·least I should be,
For I dearly delight in a wild Christmas spree,
And that good Santa Claus is my host and my friend,
And all that he does, I am here to defend.
Let no one be grave now, or wear a long face,
Else myself and friend Frolic will fly from the place:
For "to laugh and be fat" is our motto and mode,
And the gay heart of childhood's our favorite abode.
All prim little girls we dislike and detest,
So stiff and old-maidish, so mightily dressed;—
Little women of ten make a pitiful sight—
If there's any such here, let us put her to flight.
But I love honest nature, her laugh and her smile
So pleasant and sunny, yet modest the while:
So, my dear little girls, be as gay as you please,
And myself and my friend will feel quite at our ease.

FROLIC, *who has been leaning on the arm of her friend, bows*
to the audience and says:

My eloquent friend has said all I could say,
If I talked till the sunset of this merry day;
So I've only to beg you'll leave nothing undone
To follow the counsels of Frolic and Fun.

IMAGINATION *stands up, and looks wistfully at* SANTA CLAUS
at first, and, as her speech goes on, away into space, and says:

What fancies gather around me
    As I gaze upon his face,
And watch his smile and whispers,
    And all their meaning trace!
I imagine all the treasures
    E'er sought in sun-bright isles,
Where the day beams on for ever,
    And creation always smiles:

I go down, a fancied diver,
   'Mid the wine-dark Indian seas,
And gather pearls and corals
   For fair young necks like these.
The Grecian Archipelago
   I search for gems antique,
Relics of bygone splendor
   When Art could all but speak.
To Egypt's wondrous pyramids
   I take a daring flight,
And see the sacred Ibis
   So solemn, yet so bright:
But here I don't imagine
   E'en Santa Claus could find
Things portable or handy,—
   He'd leave them all behind.
He'd rather seek in China
   Rich silks and vases rare,
And curious little bijoux,
   And costly china-ware;
Or bring from queer old Jeddo
   (You know it's in Japan),
Whate'er you want well-varnished—
   A desk, a box, a fan!
But see how I have wandered!
   Excuse me, 'tis my style
Is that you, Generosity?
   I knew your gracious smile.

GENEROSITY.

Why, yes, my old acquaintance—
   I just came here to see
Our dear young friends make merry,
   'Tis real joy to me;

I'd like to make them happy,
 To sow within their hearts
The seed of every virtue,
 E'er youth's bright spring departs:
And gladly do I share in
 The pleasures of to-day,
I almost envy Santa Claus
 Who gives such bliss away.
Dear Charity, my cousin,
 My own, my chosen friend!
Tell him the "homeless children"
 On you and me depend;
And beg of him to send them
 Some candies and some cakes:
You'll find he'll kindly do it
 If only for our sakes.

CHARITY *comes forward looking very happy, and says:*
 Yes, while you all are gaily laughing,
 And the cup of pleasure quaffing—
 While the Christmas bells are ringing,
 And the Christmas songs are singing,
 While sweet Christmas faces brighten,
 Heavy hearts begin to lighten,
 Art and nature, love and life—
 All of Christmas thoughts are rife;
 And old Santa Claus comes *down*,
 Every grief in glee to drown;
 Yet I cannot choose but think
 Of the hearts in woe that sink;
 Of the poor who pine away
 Lone and cold on Christmas-day,
 Of the little children left
 Homeless, and of hope bereft;
 With their bare and tiny feet
 Frozen with the freezing sleet,

And their fair young shoulders bowed,
And their sorrow sobbing loud.—
Ah, my dear young friends! for them
Santa Claus has no bright gem.
Daily bread, *perhaps*, he'll bring,
Or a passing pleasure fling,—
Not for them, the joy, the glee
That around I gladly see;
But be *you* their Santa Claus
Winning thus most true applause.
Trifles *plenty* well may spare
Would to them be treasures rare;
Clothes to shield them from the cold,
Little books so cheaply sold,
Would make winter seem a time,
Gay to them as summer's prime.
Santa Claus, my dear old friend,
Some of your rare treasures send
To the children of the poor,
Who so many wants endure!
For the Babe of Bethlehem
Pays for all you give to them;
He was poor e'en as they are,
When arose the Magi's star.

SPEECH OF SANTA CLAUS.

I've been watching all this time
A chance to say in prose or rhyme,
How delightful it appears,
How my inmost heart it cheers,
Thus to see you gaily meet,
Your old friend Santa Claus to greet!
Sure enough, I've travelled far,
Not by any dull rail-car.
Viewless are the wings I wear,
As fair Berenice's hair;

11

And I roam o'er sea and land
As the Christmas chimes command:
Used to public speaking, I
Am *not used* to feeling shy.
But there is a presence here
That makes me feel a little queer—
'Tis not Fun, she's my old pet—
Nor Fancy, though I'll make her fret—
For I quite forgot the fans
From those isles they call Japan's.
Neither is it Expectation—
I meet with her in every nation,
Nor is it Curiosity,
Tho' a bore she is to me—
Not Generosity, tho' quite my forte—
Nor Charity, who queens my court—
Nor *you*, nor *you*, nor any
    Of all these little dames
That throng so brightly 'round me,
    With all their Christmas claims.
Oh, yes, 'tis Mother Agnes!
    'Tis she who stands apart,
With all her cherished daughters,
    That touches thus my heart!
Yes, I am well accustomed
    To this world's wild *éclat*,
For all its loud hurrahing
    I do not care a straw;
But, oh the name of *Mother!*
    So beautiful—so sweet,
All language has no other
    Could bring me to her feet—
Where kneeling down, dear children,
    I, Santa Claus, protest,

I envy you your mother,
 And call you richly blest!
Not gifts from rich Golconda
 Can match a *mother's* heart,—
Then love her—make her happy
 With love's exhaustless art.
If she will but permit me,
 My gracious right I'll waive,
She better will distribute
 The gifts dear Christmas gave;
Her hand will make them dearer,
 Her smile more sweetly cheer,—
Her words, perhaps, to Heaven
 Will draw some heart more near.
I've very far to travel,
 I'll leave you all to her,
And say farewell, though parting
 Makes old affections stir.
Though "physically forty,"
 My heart feels young once more,
For the blessed name of mother
 Thrills me as it did of yore.
Farewell, now, dearest children!
 Mother Agnes dear, farewell!
May heaven's divinest blessings
 Enchain you as a spell!
May love for ever round you
 Weave meshes of God's grace,
And bind you at life's closing
 In glory's bright embrace!
May that life, O dearest mother,
 Win the Saviour's own applause,—
May its end know naught of sorrow
 Like the reign of Santa Claus!

THE FLOWERS DISSATISFIED.

BEAN-BLOSSOM.

Good morning, dear Miss Daffodil !—
  That dashing yellow dress
Looks lovely with the green leaves,
  You think so too, I guess:
I really feel quite envious—
  My plain and sober hues
I'd willingly change with you,
  If I were free to choose.

DAFFODIL.

I know that you, Bean-Blossom,
  Have not much pomp or show,
That in your frail corollas
  No golden anthers glow;
But, sweetest friend, believe me,
  My shining dress I'd part,
With pleasure, for the perfume
  That dwells within your heart !

TULIP.

O pearl-like Orange-Blossom,
  Emblem of all that's pure ;
For you the glorious summer
  For ever shall endure !
While I, a fragile Tulip,
  Am doomed to quick decay,
Alas, these painted petals,
  How fast they fall away !

ORANGE BLOSSOM.

For shame, ungrateful creature!
  To slight your magic dyes—
Crimson and white and purple,
  Gold, like the bright sunrise :

You envy my snow petals,
   Hid 'mong this mass of green—
You, the majestic Tulip,
   The garden's chosen queen!

DAISY.

Poor me! I'm but a Daisy,
   With white and yellow hat,
And yet I'd soon be something
   If I were not so flat;
When I behold that Lilac
   Swing graceful on its bough,
I blush until the crimson
   Tinges my tips, as now!

LILAC.

Well, well! I've been admiring
   These Daisies all my life,
They look so sweet and gentle,
   So free from storm and strife;
The green grass gathers around them
   To shelter and caress—
I'm shaken by the zephyr,
   Who heeds not my distress.

WALL-FLOWER.

I wish I were a Hyacinth,
   Magnificent and rare,
But I'm a poor wild flower
   Growing on walls all bare;
And so they call me Wall-Flower,
   As if I were a stone—
I wish they'd mind their business
   And let *poor me* alone!

HYACINTH.

O silly, silly flower!
  For freedom is your own—
I'm treated as a prisoner
  From garret e'en to throne!
Beside the toilet, often,
  Of some insipid girl,
I'm fixed while she's admiring
  A diamond or a pearl.
Like romance, still you cling to
  The old historic walls,
I flaunt in open windows,
  I'm *sold* in market stalls:
Give me the breath of heaven—
  The free, the undefiled—
I'll change my fatal beauty
  With any Hedge-Rose wild.

HEDGE-ROSE.

With me! You cannot mean it?
  My lot is very hard—
My beautiful relations
  My every claim discard:
By blood I am connected
  With all the race of Rose,
Yet here I am, the plaything
  Of every wind that blows.

GARDEN-ROSE.

I know it—I admit it—
  But it is Flora's fault;
She mated you with Briars,
  I'd set her will at naught;
I'd say to her, I'm just as good
  As Moss or Monthly Rose—
I tell you, Madam Flora,
  I'd say it to your nose!

FLORA, *who has been peeping from behind something, rushes*
out in a passion and scolds them all:

Well—I declare! Did ever
Mother or mistress hear
Of conduct so ungrateful,
So *contrary*, so queer!
You, Rose! you heartless creature,
You ill-natured, spoiled pet!
I've half a mind to give you
A blow you'd ne'er forget!

ROSE.

You're kind to me—I know it;
I've perfume, color, all
Your art can give a flower—
I would my words recall;
But then you are tyrannic,
You do just as you will,
And think that we should praise you
For most consummate skill!

FLORA.

Be silent, I am empress!
I shall know how to act,
To each and all; my justice
You'll find will be exact.
Come here—you Miss Bean-Blossom—
You thankless little thing;
Although you're not a nettle,
I see that you can sting—
And you, my own chef-d'œuvre,
You, Tulip, to rebel!
The proud are all ungrateful—
I should have known it well.

TULIP.

Oh yes, my royal mistress,
  I find that you can scold,
And so could I, but really
  I find I've got a cold!
Besides you know I'm nervous,
  These petals are *so* slight—
A little more excitement
  Would shake them off outright.

FLORA.

You nervous? You're too confident,
  Too saucy, I should say;
I'll bring you to your senses
  Before you see next May:
To think how I have sheltered
  That stupid Daisy's bloom—
How little dreamed that envy
  In *her* heart could find room!

DAISY.

Dear me! my lady-mother,
  I'm smothered in this grass,
And tortured by the children,
  Who pluck me as they pass!

FLORA.

You silly thing! You know not
  The treasures you possess;
For Innocence and Modesty
  Unite your bloom to bless.
But you, my queenly Hyacinth,
  Valued by rich and poor,—
How could you murmur? Beautiful
  Your lot is, I am sure.

But so it is with mortals,
 What they can't have they prize,
While that which suits their spirit
 They foolishly despise.
Yet there are *some* exceptions:
 That pale, sweet Mignonette,
I never knew to murmur,
 Or at her hues to fret;
Nor that dear, humble Primrose
 That blooms in places lone,
The bees, her sole admirers,
 The courtiers of her throne.
The Violet hiding lowly,
 Yet pouring sweets around—
These are my pets—they never
 Ungrateful will be found.

MIGNONETTE.

Ah mother, sweetest mother!
 Forgive these foolish buds,
They are sorry—do forgive them,
 Their tears fall now in floods;
They have not reached the years when
 Discretion holds the rein—
So, mother dear, forgive them:
 Mercy becomes a queen.

PRIMROSE.

Do, mother, and we'll warrant
 That all will be content:
The Tulip with her colors,
 Bean-Blossom with her scent;
That all will be obedient
 And dutiful to you—
Look at the Rose ! she's blushing,
 And almost weeping too.
11*

ROSE.

I know I'm the most guilty—
  So I will speak for all:
Forgive us, dearest mother,
  Here at your feet we fall;
"The proud are all ungrateful,"
  But we'll be proud no more;
So take us to your bosom
  And love us *as before.*

FLORA.

Come to my heart ! I know not
  What tempted you: but now
I know 'tis all forgotten,
  No cloud is on my brow;
No shadow on my spirit,
  No sadness on my heart—
Bloom on in all your beauty,
  Summer will soon depart!
Then let us haste together
  Out to the woodlands green,
The birds will serenade us,
  The flowers and their queen;
The butterflies will greet us,
  The bees our welcome bring—
Come, children ! Let us hasten!—
  I promised this last Spring.

THE MARTYRDOM OF THE MACCABEES.

Scene First.—*A hall in Jerusalem, where arms, banners, and warlike accoutrements are mingled with many evidences of Eastern luxury.*

PRESENT:

ANTIOCHUS EPIPHANES, king of Syria.
APOLLONIUS, one of the generals of his army.
LYSIAS, a prince of the blood royal and a general also.
TIMOTHEUS and BACCHIDES, officers of the king's household.

They endeavor to excite ANTIOCHUS *to renewed cruelties, against the Jews.*

APOLLONIUS.

BEHOLD, great king, while earth and sea obey thee!
  While age, and youth, and manhood hail thy name,
While the wide Syrian Empire owns thy sceptre,
  And magnifies thy power with proud acclaim!
Behold, my king, these unsubdued Judeans,
  Sons of a strange, inexplicable race,
They do defy thee; and their proud Jehovah
  Reigns with a sway that shames thee to thy face.
Shall it be told in Antioch the peerless,
  Shall it be told along its gorgeous streets,
That *thou* art set at naught, *thy* gods dishonored,
  Thy power defied, even on its judgment seats?
O Syria, Syria, land of sun and splendor,
  Glory of earth, and favorite of the skies!
Look on your king, Antiochus! behold him,
  While a poor prostrate land his power defies!
Shall we return to tell this tale, where evening
  Wooes to thy bloomy bowers thy dark-eyed maids?

Hearing this news, methinks I see them weeping
  With haughty shame beneath thy palm-tree shades.
For now the Jews deride *us* and our arms,
  They recognize a power to us unknown;
From whom even thou, O king! but hold'st thy power,
  And who can blight the glory of thy throne.
Arise and crush these wretches thus presuming,
  Subdue them—bend their knees before thy shrines:
This earth-renowned Jerusalem shall own thee,
  Or from this day thy royal sway declines.

ANTIOCHUS.

Fool !—thou art raving.   Am I not the master,
  Monarch, and ruler of this ancient land ?
Are there enough of men of Juda living,
  Against my will one single hour to stand ?
Have I not trodden down their haughty spirits,
  Have I not quenched the fire within their hearts ?
They dare not name the God they inly worship,
  Dare not 'gainst me employ their wisdom's arts.

LYSIAS.

Hear me, my king!   Omnipotent, supernal
  Would be your sway o'er all this Eastern world,
Were but this people, who despise your sceptre,
  Into destruction's vortex quickly hurled :
Why, old men trembling on the grave's dark precincts,
  Are brave enough to laugh your laws to scorn !
Like Eleazer who defied our power
  And died rejoicingly this very morn.

ANTIOCHUS.

Aye, but he died !   We slew him in his frenzy,
  And left our names recorded in his blood :
What Jew will now refuse us his allegiance
  Here, in the presence of that crimson flood ?

LYSIAS.

Not him alone, not but his grey-haired folly,
   But even women and their children dare
Despise the great Antiochus—defy him—
   And count his mandates among things that were.
Even women! Why those maidens of Judea
   Would die in multitudes before they'd kneel
One moment at our shrines—hatred, and horror,
   And loathing for our worship—all they'd feel.

TIMOTHEUS.

The land of Abraham is surely conquered,
   But not his sons, for still our power they brave;
Jordan flows seaward, shadowed by our banners—
   But can they stay the rush of one free wave ?
Thus mind is free,—the Free Eternal Spirit
   Made it His Image and His shrine to be.
You cannot chain it. Mind will ne'er be conquered,
   Most mighty king and master, even by thee!
Therefore these girls defy us! men and children,
   And women with their babes, are proudly brave:
The soul within them will not own your shackles,
   The God *they* dream of reigns beyond the grave.
You will not conquer them, but will be conquered;—
   Pardon my truthful love that won't endure
Defeat for him I honor. Leave this people
   Their old traditions and their creed so pure:
Still let them follow Abraham and Jacob,
   Still wait the coming of the Promised One,
Still live in their antique, ideal day-dreams—
   In all things else, thy slaves they'll soon become.

ANTIOCHUS.

How have I heard this council to its closing ?
   Man! do you *dare* tell *me* I must give way

To old men, little children, simple maidens?
  Name them and let me look on them, I pray!

BACCHIDES.

My liege, 'tis true.   A woman worn and widowed,
  But with a band of noble-looking boys
Who call *her* mother, and seem sons of princes,
  Has scorned our gifts as vain and empty toys;
Nor trembles at our threats, nor dreads our fires,
  Nor fears to see those children torn away
From her maternal bosom to be mangled,
  Of desert beasts the mutilated prey.

ANTIOCHUS.

They do not fear me?   Dread not death and torture?
  Bring them before me: let this woman stand
Here in my presence!   You shall see her worship
  The gods of mine and of my father's land.
They do not fear me?   I have sacked their temple,
  Built by the guidance of inspirèd men,
And rent its veil and seized upon its treasures,
  And made its sacrifices cease.   Again
Must I renew the reign of terror,
  And quench rebellion in rebellious blood.
Bring in these wretches—they despise my power,
  And theirs shall swell the deep-ensanguined flood.

SCENE SECOND.—*Enter* CORAH, *the mother of the* MACCA-
  BEES, *led in by two rude soldiers, who place her before the
  tribunal.   Her sons are brought in immediately after.
  They are manacled, and are driven roughly forward.*
  MENETHAI, *the oldest of those present, rushes to his
  mother and attempts to support her, but is hindered by the
  fetters on his hands.   He, however, places himself in an
  attitude of protection at her right hand.* BENJAMIN,

*being very young, is without fetters, and seizes his mother's
robe, clinging to her, as if for shelter.* REUBEN, IHBAR,
NATHANIAS, *and* ISSACHAR *are placed behind the
others and close to them.*—ANTIOCHUS *speaks:*

These are but boys. They do not know their peril.
    The father of my people, I should feel
For youth entangled in romantic meshes,
    And with its follies leniently would deal.
Thou art the mother of these youths. A mother
    Has sacred instincts: she would save her own.
Offer with them sweet incense at that altar,
    And they are safe as my imperial throne.

CORAH.

Alas, my lord, I should but work their ruin!
    They are the children of my God, not mine!
They may not violate His dread commandments,
    Nor offer incense at an alien shrine.

ANTIOCHUS.

Fool that I was, to reason with a woman!
    The sight of blood will shake her courage soon:
These boys know better than to die for nothing—
    In its first years, life seems a priceless boon.
Come forward you who seem the nearest manhood!
    But say you honor Astaroth and Baal,
And own Antiochus your lord and master—
    Thou shalt be free—thou and thy brethren all.

MENETHAI.

If only treason against God can save them,
    Then they must die, must perish by my side!
A little life is a slight thing to offer
    To Him whose glory is our star and guide.

ANTIOCHUS.

We'll make the offering for you.   You shall perish
  By some unheard-of death, some pang unknown
But to the torturer's art.   For this proud folly
  Thy heart's best blood poured out shall soon atone.

MENETHAI.

King! you are master here.   Your will is potent;
  Yet can it not o'ermaster mine.   And I
For my Creator, Lord, and Sovereign Master,
  For His dear law and love, am here to die:
My life is His—His glory is my standard;
  For *it* to die is to attain true life,
Therefore my heart is ready, and I fear not
  The martyr's death—the sacrificial knife.

ANTIOCHUS.

The boy is mad! but soon the sight of torture
  Such as we deal in here shall make him tame;
Let him die many deaths—make him the terror
  Of all that worship this Jehovah's name.

EXECUTIONER.

How shall we torture him, most clement master ?
  Decree his fate, and he shall meet it soon.
By fire or sword, or suddenly, or slowly,
  So slowly he shall count life's close a boon ?

ANTIOCHUS.

Babbler, begone, and do your cursed office !
  Devise new agonies, as you know how;
Torture him slowly, and be sure to spare him
  When he consents to Baal the knee to bow.

MENOTHAI.

God of my fathers ! by *their* faith I swear it,
  Ne'er shall I kneel to honor aught but Thee!
God of my fatherland! death would be glory,
  If that dear land it could at last set free.
Oh, by the memory of the faith of Abraham,
  By Isaac's love, Jacob's prophetic lore;
By our sweet mother Rachel,—Ruth the faithful,
  By all the patriarchs and priests of yore,
Help the old land! Dear Lord, Almighty Father,
  Renew thy covenant, protect Thine own :
Destroy these pagan tyrants. Let our sorrow
  For all our sinfulness and pride atone.

ANTIOCHUS.

Lead him away to torture, to destruction!
  Shut that insulting mouth with molten lead!
Bring out the desert-beasts and let their craving
  With the hot blood of his base veins be fed!

  He is seized and hurried off by the executioners.

SCENE THIRD.—ZEBULON, *the oldest of the family, here*
  rushes into the hall, having met in the vestibule the officers
  who dragged his brother to the torture, and having been
  directed to his mother by the words of MENETHAI, *who*
  called to him as he passed. Overpowered by his feelings, he
  does not even notice the presence of the king, but leaning
  against a column for support in his agony, addresses his
  mother :

Mother! my own loved mother! mother gentlest,
  Most honored, best-beloved, and most dear!
O mother, mother! have I fondly sought thee
  Only to find thee in this place of fear ?
Friend of my heart! sister as well as mother,
  Are my hands helpless that they cannot aid

Thee in thy dread, dark sorrow ?—Am *I* living,
  And thou to death and agony betrayed ?
I that have known no sorrow, *no* heart-rending,
  But thy kind voice hath soothed it ; and thy soul,
Responsive to thy child's, hath drawn it gently
  Within the circle of thy sweet control!
Ah, mother, mother! all the past is with me,
  Its agonizing throes, its wild despair;
O sovereign lady of my life, how often
  Had I been lost but for thy tender care!
Our years were full of torture: life came to me
  Just when the sorrows of our land were worst;
It brought me but a dower of desolation—
  Thy loved hand held me from being all accursed.
Why must the chain that bound our hearts be broken ?
  "That bound," I said ?—that binds and binds for aye;
That holds our hearts together and will hold them
  Till life's poor light is quenched,—its feeble ray
  Lost in the splendor of eternal day.
Then let the torture come—death do its utmost ;
  Let pain life's utmost energies o'ertask,
But, Lord, take Thou our mother's gentle spirit!
  Save *her* from this brute death! 'tis all I ask.
Let no rude hand approach her: close her eyelids
  By some sweet doom, and then we are Thine own.
My brave boy-brothers ! let their young blood flowing
  Win them a place near to Thy glory's throne.

He clasps his hands in an agony of prayer and is silent. One
  of the executioners, at a sign from the king, who had im-
  patiently expected an appeal for mercy, while the martyr
  spoke, seizes and binds him. He is immediately
  dragged to the sacrifice. REUBEN *is then brought*
  forward, and the remaining brothers press close to
  their mother, who had sunk on her knees during the
  prayer of ZEBULON, *and evidently prays herself.* LYSIAS,

directed by the king to endeavor to intimidate the martyr,
speaks:

Now then, young Israelite, bow down and worship
   The gods your king commands you to adore;
Bend that proud head and sacrifice to Baal,
   Or mingle yours with your vile brother's gore.

REUBEN.

Oh freely let it flow! and freely mingle
   With his, the glory of our house, its pride;
Like him, I worship but the God of Jacob:
   Lead me to him—he cannot yet have died.
Fain would I die with him, my glorious brother,
   So stalwart, and so noble, and so true:
These are but boys, they acted at our bidding;
   Spare them, and let the victims be us two.
Ah, my heart softens as I gaze upon thee,
   Mother, with these thy children at thy side:
Spare them—they cannot die so full of beauty!
   Mercy should be to monarchs as a bride.

ANTIOCHUS.

Why, we should gladly spare their lives and freely?
   'Tis you who write their sentence, boy, not we;
Place them before the shrine of Baal Peor
   With incense in their hands—and they are free.

REUBEN.

God of my fathers! thou behold'st them kneeling,
   The last, the very last of all our race;
For Thee they come to die, our God, our Father,
   And for the glory of thy dwelling place!
Thou art a man, Antiochus—a mortal;
   A higher law than thine was made for me:
I die for love of Him who gave me being,
   Not at the fiat of a thing like thee.

ANTIOCHUS.

Bear him away, and end these mock heroics!
  Tear him to pieces,—crush his haughty heart.
A higher law than mine!—Vile dog of Juda!
  Torture him men! exhaust on him your art !

APOLLONIUS.

My lord and king, this process seems too tedious!
  Art thou not weary of this sickening scene ?
Yon brother-fools begin at last to tremble,
  I'll place them where their compeers just have been ;
Then let them choose the death they seem to covet,
  Or own the gods we worship and adore.
[*In a low voice.*]
  Are they not noble youths, so proud and fearless ?
  I would give countless sums to win them o'er.

ANTIOCHUS.

It is too true! There's more of truth and honor
  Within their hearts than kindles in their eyes.
Accursed laws that keep aloof such subjects!
  The very gods they're made for I despise.
I am their master. They must own my sceptre;
  I'll make them worship even things of dust,
Such as their flesh is made of, if I please it:
  Bow down and honor me they shall, they must.
[*Addressing the Martyrs.*]
  Life is yet young in these hot veins: bethink you
  Of the long years of glory you may win
As soldiers of Antiochus. Let Juda
  The tide of misery she courts drink in.
Choose ye a better fate: be men, not madmen,
  Wildly to sell your life-blood for a dream,—
An old, effete, absurd, uncompromising,
  Self-sacrificing faith, that knows no mean.

Speak! I see reason reasserts her power—
  Say you are mine.   Bend but to honor me—
I represent the gods and all the powers:
  Speak but one word of fealty and you're free.

ISSACHAR.

Blood of my brethren! Ah, you call too loudly;
  We cannot hear a meaning in the voice,
That spake your doom; the voice that vainly bids us
  Embrace destruction as our spirit's choice:
Yes, haughty Syrian! life is young within us,
  And the strong spirit of our fathers free;
Free, though our limbs are shackled, we can bend them,
  To death for God's dear love—but not to thee.
Mother, farewell! we meet where death comes never,
  Beyond the confines of time's surging sea;
God's glory is our watchword, faith our buckler—
  Now, God of Abraham, we come to thee!

ANTIOCHUS.

Lead them away in silence; crush them slowly
  With deadly weights into a mass of death:
These three together.   Let them know no mercy,
  No respite, till they yield that daring breath.
[*In a low voice.*]
I'll try the woman now, her heart is broken—
  She'll cling with wild affection to that boy —
He's half a child.   She cannot see him tortured:
  That form of his seems made of light and joy.

BACCHIDES.

First try the boy.   He's obstinate; I see it
  In the dark gleam of those proud Hebrew eyes:
Young as he is, he'd trample on our standard—
  The might of all our armies he defies.

There is no way to crush these Jews but kill them;
  They only fear dishonor, only dread
To sin against Jehovah. Thus you see them
  Rejoice the while they go to join the dead.
But let us try. This people will despise us
  If even a child we cannot force to yield;
I'll offer him dominion, power, glory:
  Tell him his country he may save and shield.
[*Addresses* BENJAMIN.]
  Come, boy of Israel! another Joseph,
    Perhaps in Syria's palaces you'll reign,
  Even as he did in Egypt! Life, and splendor,
    And power, and glory you may yet attain.

ANTIOCHUS.

We would not crush so fresh and fair a flower,
  We would not stop the beating of that heart;
Nor cast to cruel beasts a life that only
  Begins on earth's fair scenes its pleasant part.
Come, then, and worship Baal—'tis but a form:
  Fling but the incense on that leaping flame,
And cast away the trappings of your people,
  And seek the glory of a Syrian name.

BENJAMIN.

Alas, my Lord, I love my own Judea,
  I love her flowery valleys and her hills:
But I must die. Death calls me to my brothers.
  Death! What is death? Its name my bosom chills.

BACCHIDES.

Aye, what is death ? Say rather what is torture,
  And shame, and infamy ? for all are yours:
To die the prey of some huge forest monster,
  This is what folly like your own insures.

BENJAMIN.

O my sweet brothers, did ye die thus torn ?
  Did the wild beasts delight in your hearts' blood ?
Would I had died the first! Alas, my mother,
  Let me die here, and now—here where they stood.

CORAH.

Respice cœlum! Oh, look up, look onward;
  Onward to where heaven's radiance lights the day.
Respice cœlum! Chosen one of Juda,
  Look up, and take to heaven your glorious way;
Look up, look onward. Death is nothing real:
  The spirit never dies; the life but leaves
Its fragile earthly dwelling for a little—
  'Tis but a foolish grief for this that grieves.
"There was a voice in Rama: Rachel mourning
  Because her children were no more." But I,
I say to thee, my youngest born, my last one—
  Heaven is in view. Be brave, be calm, and die.
[*Speaks to herself in a low heart-broken tone.*]
He is so fair. That face is like a story:
  I see in it the beauty of them all.
My young fair boy, my only one, my darling!—
  Dare I those words of daring faith recall ?
O, my sweet child! that nestled in my bosom,
  A little while ago with such a love—
How shall I let him go ? My blessed children,
  Pray that your mother's spirit soar above;
That she may gather up her best affections,
  Blent as they are with her heart's inmost life,
And make of that warm heart a bleeding victim,
  Plunge in herself the sacrificial knife.

APOLLONIUS.

We'll do it for you: don't be too heroic;
  You've nothing left to live for that I know—

This boy "so fair," whose "face seems like a story,"—
We'll let you see him die just for a show.

ANTIOCHUS.

Take them away together! Let them perish,
And let their fate be told o'er all the land—.
From Dan to Beersheba, from Hermon's valleys,
To where the Jordan flows, with soft winds fanned.

*The mother catches the boy convulsively to her bosom, and ex-
claims:*

Farewell, my boy, my beautiful, my darling!
Gift of my God, my young heroic child;
Proudly I give thee to Him all untarnished,
Thy spirit free, thy young heart undefiled.
Farewell, my old ancestral home, where evening
Came in its soft and shadowy light to bow
In the deep hush of worship the young spirits
Who watch above me from the heavens now:
Alas, my eldest born, so proud and fearless,
With such a passionate, young buoyant heart—
His step was like a monarch's, and his bearing;
Yet was he filled with true affection's art.
He is a child again. His bright hair curling
Beneath the culture of his mother's hand,
The soft round cheek knows only smiles,—the lustre
Of that dark eye has something of command.
Alas, the loving hearts that grew together,
Like blossoms that are born of one green stem,
That pour their wealth of fragrance o'er each other.
Each with its pure heart kept like priceless gem.
Gentlest wert thou, the votary of the Temple!
Gentle and thoughtful with a quiet heart
And a true spirit, though subdued and saddened
By all the woes in which thy race had part.

A child of promise, lovely in thy cradle,
  Thou hadst thy mother's spirit and her face;
Not the strong nature of thy haughty fathers,
  But the religious quiet of her race.
Blessed be thou my child; and thou art blessed:
  My solace and my consolation thou.
But thou art gone! thy place is in the heavens;
  The martyr's crown upon that calm, white brow.
And thou, my own, young, radiant, joyous hopeful,
  With wit and mirth to light those speaking eyes;
Are the dead leaves already scattered o'er thee,
  Has life so *soon* cast off its thin disguise?
Back through a hundred scenes of joy and sorrow
  Flashes the busy memory that is mine;
In each the torch of love I see thee bearing.
  Lighting my life with that dear smile of thine.
My sympathizing child, deep-hearted, gentle,
  With few to share the treasure of thy love,
How much heroic truth thy gay heart sheltered,
  How much to fit thee for the realms above!.
Ah, there was one as gentle as a woman,
  With a sweet face that would not speak of woe,
And a white marble forehead that was gleaming
  With very fairness like new-fallen snow.
Sylphlike and slight, so girl-like and so lovely,
  A flowery vine that clings to some strong tree;
A bird that uttered songs of silver sounding,
  That loved its cage and sought not to be free.
A creature with no self to mar its pureness,
  That lived for others, and for others gave
His own young heart to sorrow; and then meekly
  Bore his life's load with spirit still, yet brave.
Another—yes, one more—the one that early
  Gave his whole heart to God, and God alone;

12

Whose baby lips spoke worship, and whose spirit
  Sought rest but in the shadow of the Throne.
He was my own,—peculiarly I loved him
  As friend and child and helpmate, e'en as all
That heart can be to heart; for the same sorrow
  Shadowed us both as a funereal pall.
I was his mother: care and early sorrow
  Weighed down my spirit 'neath their dark control;
But he, with that young kingly heart, was ever
  Near, with aspiring thoughts to lift my soul.
I cradled his young beauty in my bosom;
  I watched it grow and bloom—and he is gone!
God of my fathers! unto Thee I gave them:
  Now let me meet them at Thy mercy's throne!
Respice cælum.   O my child, my last one!
  Together let us scale its crimson heights;
God's glorious vision waits us at its portals,
  And our eternal home with radiance lights.

[*The executioners having returned to the hall at this moment,
  seize upon the mother and child and lead them to death.
  The court breaks up.*]

BEATRICE; OR, TEMPTATION AND TRIUMPH.

BEATRICE, *alone, soliloquizes.*

COURAGE, my soul! The world is full of beauty,
  And love, and light, and joy, and pleasant peace.
We've tried the narrow path, too long, too vainly:
  Now from its trammels shall we claim release.
Fool that I was! I sought for *rest* in labor,
  I sought for peace in painful, weary ways;
I bade thee crush thy youth's first gay aspirings,
  And made thee suffer weary nights and days.
I bade thee seek a goal divine, supernal,
  And found that disappointment was thy lot:

Holiness, God's sweet love, His joyous service
   We sought; but oh, my soul, we found them not!
Now the bright world is ours, its wild glad freedom,
   Its riches and its pleasures are our own:
Seize on them bravely. Let the past, forgotten,
   Die, that no shadow o'er our path be thrown.
Fashion, its wondrous flights of frolic, fancy,
   We'll follow as the glittering mazes whirl;
The dance, the song, the revel gay and thoughtless,
   Shall prove me, once again, a joyous girl.
Silence, my soul! Alas, why whisper sadly
   Of God's dear love and His commandments sweet;
Of Mary's mother-help, of the bright angels ?
   Silence! these thoughts are dead, they do not sleep.
There is no love eternal. All this virtue,
   This sacrifice heroic is untrue;
I would it were as childhood idly fancied,
   And I could fly, dear Angel Guide, to you.

ANGEL GUARDIAN *appears and says.*
Creature of God! His child! behold me near thee,
   In this dark hour, when Satan's deadly wile—
Would lead thee to thy ruin and beguile thee
   Thus with the semblance of the world's sweet smile;
Would hide in Faith's bright lamp and blindly lead thee
   Far from the path that leads to Jesus' feet;
Would hush the voice of conscience and persuade thee
   That foolish, fleeting joys are bliss complete.
Oh, let the true soul speak ! Grasp all the graces
   Thy baptism gave thee claim to, ere they've passed
On to some other heart, more true, more faithful:
   See, 'tis for thee these treasures were amassed.

BEATRICE.
O Angel! Angel! Is it true ? Can ever,
   Ever this faithless heart come back to Him—

The God it scoffed at—to the Truth Eternal—
  Soiled as it is, its lustre stained and dim ?

ANGEL.

Behold! the Holy Spirit in His mercy,
  And love, and infinite compassion, sends
His choicest gift to save and sanctify thee:
  Thou may'st again be numbered with His friends.

ANGEL OF THE GIFT OF WISDOM.

Again I come to thee, though oft rejected,
  To point the way to peace; to guide thee on,
Upward and onward to thy Heavenly country—
  There shalt thou find true peace, and there alone.
I come to bid thee see—see what is real,
  And true, and beautiful, and wholly good;
What is the soul's true dignity—its value,
  By men so fearfully misunderstood.
I come to deaden every evil passion,
  Exalt the understanding, cure the heart;
I come once more, soul purchased by the Saviour,
  To make thee love and choose "the better part."

BEATRICE.

Too late! too late! for I have freely chosen
  The lovely things of sense—the sun, the shade;
The beautiful of earth, its joys and pleasures;
  And I abide the choice: 'tis made—'tis made!

GUARDIAN ANGEL.

Oh speak not thus! The Gift of Understanding,
  Which I invoke, will teach thee better things;
Will form within thy mind a truer judgment,
  Will show thee whence this choice unworthy springs.

GIFT OF UNDERSTANDING.

Angel, I come! for I am sent to aid thee
  In thy sweet task of saving this dear soul;
I come to make more evident Faith's teachings,
  To point more clearly to life's destined goal.

BEATRICE.

Alas, dear Angel! all in vain this seeking,
  To lift my eyes up to that viewless world
Youth loved to dream of, ere its hopes were shattered:
  The banner of its faith is darkly furled.

ANGEL GUARDIAN.

Oh, Knowledge, Gift divine! come, make this creature
  Learn why its faith is dead—its hope a dream;
Show her the reason, dark, and deeply hidden—
  Prove that Time's treasures are not what they seem.

GIFT OF KNOWLEDGE.

Read thine own conscience. List to its complainings,
  Consider why you thus reject the true,
The good, the beautiful, the real;
  The ways thy God would lead thee to pursue.
Read and repent—kneel down and be heart-stricken,
  Knowing thy sins, thy follies, thy deceit;
Thy self-deceit, thy early graces squandered—
  Thou shalt find *sorrow* then with *bliss* replete.

BEATRICE.

Conscience! too dreadful is the voice it utters;
  Too heavy its demands, too great the price
'Twould make me pay for hope, for peace, for freedom:
  Its every boon would cost a sacrifice.

GIFT OF COUNSEL.

Yet list its summons now, when God thus calls thee,
  Now, when His will so clearly is made known;
Now is the time—act up to present graces:
  Conform to His designs, defeat thine own:
And thus you cannot err—your soul's salvation,
  Its happiness eternal, is God's will:
Faith, Wisdom, Knowledge, all conspire to help thee,
  And Counsel brings thee its divinest skill.

BEATRICE.

Veni, Creator Spiritus! Oh Veni—
  My heart is weak, it trembles at its task;
How shall I bend proud nature's wayward spirit?
  How make the sacrifices grace would ask?

ANGEL GUARDIAN.

Ah, there is aid! Aid ready, strong, and copious—
· The royal Gift of Fortitude is here;
Gift that makes saints, and martyrs, and confessors:
  That masters joy and overpowers fear.

GIFT OF FORTITUDE.

Dear soul, distrust thyself! for thou art nothing,
  But trust thy God in whom thou canst do all;
Trust to His love, His help, His grace supernal—
  His arm will ne'er withdraw to let thee fall.
He hath cast down the mighty, and hath lifted
  The humble up to summits crowned with light—
Light from the inner Heaven—and hath sent them
To preach to kings and people, and to suffer
  Great things for him who still defends the right.
Behold St. Agnes, child of thirteen summers,
  Bravely lay down her life for Jesus' sake;

St. Philomene, in girlhood's brilliant morning,
  Her place among the martyrs nobly take!
Behold the poor of Christ! In peace they suffer,
  In lands heretical, for faith alone;
And cold and want, and homelessness and exile
  Endure, to keep their place before God's throne.
Cast down, then, emulously, all these idols,
  That self-love worships with such ardent zeal;
Be what your conscience bids you; God but values
  That which you are and do—not what you feel!

BEATRICE.

"That which I am and do!" Alas, sweet spirit,
  What am I but a poor, weak, sinful child,
What have I done but evil—will God bear me
  In His dread Presence—I, so sin-defiled?
Amplius lava me! Dear Lord, oh cleanse me,
  Wash all these earth stains in Thy blood away;
Back to my childhood's faith I come—but sadly
  For I have lost the grace, the power to pray.

GIFT OF PIETY.

Up to the Father of all consolation,
  The God of Mercy, lift thy dazzled eyes:
His love, His tenderness, His fond compassion
  Will fill thy soul with a most sweet surprise.
Then will the voice of prayer break forth harmonious;
  Thanksgiving and the sound of praise be heard;
As I myself will teach thee prayer, more grateful,
  More touching than if thou had'st never erred.

BEATRICE.

Oh, so much blessedness I dare not dream of!
  Penance and shuddering fear is now my doom;
And nevermore to lift my eyes to Heaven,
  Till death has wrapped me in its awful gloom.

GIFT OF FEAR.

Nay, speak not thus! you wrong God's loving bounty,
  Which giveth freely and upbraideth not;
The Fear of God is hopeful, filial, gentle,
  It brightens and makes sweet the hardest lot.
Quiet reserve, a sort of holy trembling,
  And a great horror of the least offence
Belong to it: but do not crush the spirit
  Nor the aspirings of God's love immense.

ANGEL GUARDIAN.

Courage and strength and happiness together,
  Dear soul, shall come to elevate your life
Into a better and a loftier region—
  Nerve and sustain you in this painful strife.
Faith, with the beauty of its revelations,
  Hope, with unfailing cheerfulness and trust;
Love, love divine, true fount of bliss, shall bring thee
  Graces to lift thy spirit from the dust.

BEATRICE.

"Faith, hope, and love divine!" Alas, I wasted
  In days now gone their treasures, and I feel
A dismal want within my inmost being:
  A want that makes my brain grow sick and reel.

FAITH.

Long hidden in thy heart and long neglected,
  I come to animate thy soul anew;
To clear away the mists of doubt and show thee
  God's word, immutable and always true;
To tell creation's story and redemption's;
  To point to Calvary's dear cross, and say
That Jesus died to save thee, and that Mary
  Is here, to help you on your heavenward way:

That sacrament and sacrifice appointed
    Are meant to save and sanctify your soul;
That God is merciful, and just, and loving,
    And reigneth mightily from pole to pole.
In all thy wanderings I have never left thee,
    Within thy heart unknown and all unseen
I kept my lamp still trimmed : a child of Mary—
    I knew thee once, entrusted to Heaven's queen.
Believe and be at rest : lay haughty reason
    Down in humility at Jesus' feet;
And to His law supreme pay solemn homage,
    Then shalt thou find a peace serene and sweet.

HOPE.

A peace serene and tranquil, calm and holy,
    For I shall fill thy heart with pure delight,
With glad anticipations of the future,—
    Th' eternal day, that never can know night.
I promise thee all graces and all blessings
    To aid thee while thy trial-day shall last;
I'll fill thy soul with such a joyous longing
    For God's dear love, as shall efface the past.

CHARITY.

Beatrice!—soul, whom Christ hath out of thousands
    Called from the thoughtless multitude to be
His own especial servant, saved and pardoned—
    With what a wealth of love I come to thee !
I come to sanctify thy fond affections,
    To purify, to elevate them all,
To make thee love all whom thy Saviour died for,
    To make thee docile to his love's sweet call.
What if thy neighbor, weak and erring, chill thee,
    With cold or cutting words, or want of love—
Hast thou not also sinned ? and he is destined
    To share with thee a glorious home above.

I come to make thee serve him, love him, bless him,
  For sake of that dear Lord who loves him well,
And richens oft his soul with sacramental,
  Supernal grace beyond what words can tell.
But most I come to teach thy heart to love Him,
  Thy God, thy Saviour and thy soul's true friend;
To teach thy soul the spirit of atonement
  Made sweet by love.—love such as cannot end.
I come to call thee to the heart of Jesus,
  The Sacred Heart, that gave its life-blood all,
To make thee what thou art.—Oh, be thou faithful!
  Grace will not twice repeat this loud heart-call.

BEATRICE.

I come, I come! oh wisdom blessed wisdom!
  Sweet gift that oped my heart to all this grace;
To hope and faith, and love of God—all blessings
  Came with the shining of thy heavenly face.
Dear guardian of my soul! O glorious Angel!
  How hast thou saved and shielded me so long;
How hast thou gained for me such priceless blessings,
  Graces so beautiful, so pure, so strong?
How shall I thank thee, if in bliss for ever
  In God's dear charity I learn to live:
Loving and worshipping His tender mercy—
  Angel to thee, what praises shall I give?

Here the ANGEL *unveils an image of* MARY, *leads* BEATRICE
  to its feet, and says:

"Not unto me, not unto me, give glory,"
  Your mother gave you, infant as you were, .
Into our Lady's bosom; and in dying,
  Entrusted you to her most tender care.
I had been sent to be your Guardian Spirit,
  But oh! so oft rejected was my aid

That I had sought some soul more true, more faithful,
  Had I not known our Lady for you prayed.
Now, you are hers again; again rejoicing,
  I lead my child, thus to her blessed feet—
Temptation's hour was dark, and dire, and deadly:
  The triumph is with greater joy replete.

     [BEATRICE *remains kneeling, and the curtain drops.*]

THE EMBASSY OF THE ANGELS.

ENVOY OF THE GUARDIAN ANGELS.

FROM the far heavens, from eternal splendors,
  I come with messages of peace and prayer;
I come to point the pathway that leads thither,
  And guide you to it, with a mother's care.
That path is called Humility; upon it
  Graces are falling like the morning dew;
And virtues sweet and patient grow and flourish,
  Cold hearts grow warm, and even false ones true.
We Guardian Angels all delight to tread it;
  Princes of Heaven, we love to serve on earth
The souls that Jesus died for, and to guard them
  Through all life's ways e'en from their day of birth.
So now in aid of dear St. Joseph's homestead,
  We make this offering from the Guardian choir;
Praying that God may bless the work and aid it,
  And with His grace its friends may all inspire.

ENVOY OF THE ARCHANGELS.

Those paths will lead to Heaven, if deeds of mercy
  And pious charity perfume the way:
Archangels send me to instil this doctrine
  On this sweet evening in Our Lady's May.

To tell you charity knows how to cover
    A multitude of sins, from God's clear view;
That mercy for the merciful is waiting,
    That penance can a sinful heart renew.
Our duty is to aid the Church's princes,
    To help the Holy Father, bishops all;
Yet children of our Queen, we pray that ever
    Blessings may sweetly on your household fall.

ENVOY OF THE PRINCIPALITIES.

Be sure such acts are done for God's dear glory,
    That pure intention sanctify them all;
Else on the judgment day, alas, how vainly
    E'en works of mercy will you then recall!
From the bright principalities, who over
    Empires, and kingdoms, and republics, keep
Their angel-guard, I come, by them deputed
    To teach this truth so simple, yet so deep.
This truth that all our works should be for Jesus,
    Be done for Him and in His holy grace;
That thus they satisfy for sin, and gain you,
    In His bright heaven, a more than glorious place.

ENVOY OF THE POWERS.

This work is hard to human hearts: for ever
    The tempter darkly seeks to interpose
Shadows 'twixt man and God—to mix with evil
    All that he says or does, or thinks, or knows.
But God, all-wise, all-powerful, all-seeing,
    Sends *us*, the Powers, to overthrow his force;
To break his snares, to sunder the dark networks
    He weaves as he pursues his deadly course.
So I, the envoy of the choir of Powers,
    Come to assure you of my constant care;
For Mary is our queen, and Mary's children
    Are all the objects of our earnest prayer.

To Mary, therefore, as the spouse of Joseph,
  A prayer we offer for sweet Mercy's home,
Where safe in Mercy's lap, dear homeless children
  May rest, no longer in distress to roam.

ENVOY OF THE VIRTUES.

Yes, but then life itself is full of dangers,
  Nature was cursed when very near its source;
Man meets a thousand risks, and so the Virtues
  Come to sustain him with angelic force.
The choir of Virtues can control the tempest,
  It rules the lightning, makes the thunders hush;
That still this planet keeps its flowery vesture,
  Seems wondrous, as of old the burning bush.
'Tis because, bearing the Creator's fiat,
  We say, "Thus far, no farther shalt thou go!"
Thou, ever-sweeping ocean! thou, dread earthquake!
  Shalt let thy lava only thus far flow.
To aid St. Joseph's home, we gladly offer
  Our help, well knowing 'twill oppose his reign
Who is God's enemy, and yours—for ever
  Seeking bright innocence with guilt to stain.

ENVOY OF THE DOMINATIONS.

Zeal for God's glory, love of souls consumes us,
  Our joy and our delight is his dear will:
Sinners, dear sinners, Jesus died to save you,
  And lived to teach you with divinest skill.
Children, your innocence is but His purchase;
  O treasure—it is God's most precious gift!
Safe in St. Joseph's home, your Mother Mary
  Your pure hearts to the *Sacred Heart* will lift.
O Joseph, friend of Jesus, spouse of Mary!
  We, Dominations, call you to our aid;
Ask you with us to labor for the children,
  That they may not to evil be betrayed.

ENVOY OF THE THRONES.

"Peace upon earth," peace to God's chosen servants,
　"Men of good will," hearts generous and true;
Peace such as God bestows we come to wish you,
　God's glory and his love alone in view.
Peace, patience, penance, perseverance ever,
　We ask for those who pray to us for aid;
That with these graces rich they may be faithful
　To Jesus Christ, in sunshine as in shade.
The Thrones have sent me here, for them to offer
　This contribution for St. Joseph's home;
Joyous I left the glorious courts of heaven,
　On this sweet mercy-errand here to come.

ENVOY OF THE CHERUBIM.

Knowledge and light enkindle in the bosoms
　Of the eighth choir of angels such deep fear,
Such awe-struck love and reverence, that seldom
　Beyond the inner heaven do they appear:
Yet now, that very knowledge bears them earth-ward,
　Makes them look down on dear St. Joseph's home;
For well they know how deeply Jesus loves them,
　Those little ones who now unsheltered roam.
They know with what a love the Eternal Father
　Regards the souls for which the Sacred Heart
Of His dear Son expended all its life-blood—
　And pray they may not from its love depart.
And so the Cherubim depute me to you,
　This offering for the children's home to make;
Praying the Holy Spirit to protect all
　Who labor for it, for sweet Jesus' sake.

ENVOY OF THE SERAPHIM.

"Love, and do all that love can do and suffer,"
　Said the great saint of love, Augustine grand;

Love, and your soul is saved, your sins forgiven;
Love, and you join in Heaven the chosen band.
Love is our life: we live in love of Jesus,
Of God the Father, of the Spirit Blest;
And for God's love, we love the little children,
And love to call them to their heavenly rest.
Oh ye who love, who for God's Holy Mother,
And dear St. Joseph labor with such zeal,
To build that home, where the sweet love of Jesus,
Will teach each heart fraternal love to feel,—
We pray for you, we offer to our Lady
Your every prayer, all gladly in your name;
And ask our Lord that *love* of Him may kindle
Each heart among you with its ardent flame.

ANGEL OF THE IMMACULATE CONCEPTION.

Blessed Angels, dear companions,
Hear the wondrous tale I tell:
How the Virgin Mother's spirit
Was kept pure, when nature fell.
When the fatal sin of Adam
Sent its evil through the veins
Of all mankind, like the life-blood,
Heritage of woes and pains;
I was sent to shield her bosom
From its virus sharp and strong;
She the chosen Mother-Virgin,
Queen of Heaven's ecstatic throng.
Still my mission is to serve her,
And my glory is to bring
Pure young hearts as her attendants,
Free like her, to Heaven's King.
Gather round your glorious Lady,
Children's heart her dearest prize;

Offer these, with her, to Jesus,
    May-flowers pleasing to His eyes!
Dear St. Joseph's Home shall hold them,
    Lilies gathered from the wild,
Flowers blushing all uncultured,
    Treasures dear to Mary's Child.
Consecrate them to her service,
    Her Sodality within;
Bind them to their Mother closely,
    Thus to keep them free from sin.
All your prayers I gladly gather,
    Offering them for Christ's dear love;
Praying Mary to reward you
    With her prayers in heaven above.

ANGEL OF ST. AGNES.

'Tis long, 'tis very long, dear friends and faithful,
    Since I addressed to you a loving word;
Since hymn or song of mine you heard, or story,
    Here, where so many hearts have loved the Lord.
'Tis long! for she who bore my name and loved me,
    Has long been gathered to her glorious rest,
Although her name in loving tones is spoken
    By those she drew to her maternal breast:
Yet in that name, I come, I come, to urge you
    To save the children for our Lord's dear sake;
To build St. Joseph's Home to be a garden,
    Where children's love the choicest scent will make.
A martyr for God's love, I long to see it
    Kindled and burning in the pure of heart:
I was a child, a girl of thirteen summers,
    When I was called to choose the martyr's part.
Dear Mother Agnes founded in this convent
    The dear Sodality of Mary's love;

To honor her Immaculate Conception,
  As the bright angels do in Heaven above.
To call on you, dear friends, and dearer sisters,
  To follow her example, and to bind
These youthful hearts to Mary's holy service,
  Where peace and truth and happiness they'll find.

PERSONIFICATION.

Characters.
MADAME LEARNING.

Her Daughters:

ORTHOGRAPHY.	ETYMOLOGY.	RHETORIC.
SYNTAX.	BOTANY.	HISTORY.
PHILOSOPHY.	ARITHMETIC.	GEOGRAPHY.

Her Enemies:
FOLLY, IGNORANCE.

Her Friend:
RELIGION.

MADAME LEARNING.

I BEG to be allowed the honor of introducing myself and daughters to this august assembly. My name is Learning—Madame Learning, of No. 1 Philosophy Place, Intelligence Street, Literary City. State of Progression. The young persons you see around me are all my daughters, yet, strange to say, their pursuits are widely different, and scarcely two of them agree either in taste or dispositions. Astronomy, one of my eldest girls, frequently separates herself from earthly pursuits entirely,

and soars away into the very heavens, while Botany
retires into the quiet country and occupies herself among
the buds and flowers. Nevertheless, there is a perfectly
good understanding between them; and Botany, as being
the younger, often consults her sister as to the supplies
of light and heat to be expected under certain circum-
stances.

So it is with them all; they differ, yet they agree, or
rather, they agree to differ. However, as they are all of
age, and I am anxious to introduce them into society,
"to bring them out," as the phrase is, I shall let them
speak for themselves. I must warn you, my friends,
against the machinations of two enemies of mine; one of
whom is openly and honestly opposed to me, while the
other endeavors to bring both myself and my children
into disrepute, by mimicking us in the most ridiculous
manner. The persons to whom I allude are named
Ignorance and Folly; and I grieve to say that I have
reason to fear that one, if not both of them, will make
some attempt to disturb the harmony of this social meeting, and, as they are perfect strangers to all present, I
thought I would put you on your guard.

Orthography, my child, come forward!—you have
always been a favorite with me, although I know you do
not attract much notice from others.

ORTHOGRAPHY.

My name is plain Orthography:
  My friends, you will agree
That none of you without my aid
  Would know the *A, B, C.*
Without me what is language?
  It lives in sound alone;
And cannot send ideas,
  Like light from zone to zone.

Without me, the astronomer
  His starry lore must hide;
The poet can but sing his odes,
  Like music by his side.
Without me, what would "Webster" be,
  Or "Walker" famed of old ?
Without me, science could but speak—
  Indeed, perhaps, she'd scold.
So here, I take my place in front,
  I'm little, but I'm strong;
And if there's any thing I hate,
  'Tis when you use me wrong.

ETYMOLOGY *comes forward hastily, and says:*

Dear me, dear me! I never can
  Have patience with such stuff!
My name is Etymology,
  That's saying quite enough:
To think that dull Orthography,
  A baby study, thus
Should rank herself before me,
  And get up such a fuss.
She simply deals in letters,
  And scarce will tell you why
She places them or here or there,
  Puts two *E*'s to spell *eye*.
For me, I scan the roots of things,
  Their origin, their course;
I trace the lineage of a word,
  Up to its primal source.
No language is *too* dead for me,
  E'en hieroglyphic lore;
I spend whole nights delighted,
  As o'er its wealth I pore.

From ancient Sanscrit writings
　　So difficult to reach,
I pass to Indian dialects
　　And modern modes of speech:
If souls but labored for God's love,
　　As I do o'er a word,
The Church would canonize more saints
　　To glorify the Lord.

SYNTAX.

Well, only hear!　You'd really think
　　These two owned half the world,
To see them thus come forward,
　　Their colors all unfurled;
While I, without whose timely aid
　　One sentence they can't speak,
Am set aside, as people treat
　　My friend, the ancient Greek.
But I won't bear it!　I am here,
　　Dame Syntax, long renowned—
Without whom Cicero was mute,
　　And Tasso ne'er was crowned;
Without whom all the classic lore
　　Were but a thing of thought,
And all my scientific friends
　　Were just as good as naught.
Without me, *subjects* cannot *act*
　　Nor predicates exist;
Without me words are nonsense all,
　　However long the list.
To Learning's self I now appeal
　　She knows the work I do;
And, as my mother, will defend
　　My cause against these two.

LEARNING.

Divide and conquer is the motto of the enemy of all union and charity, for he knows by long experience, that, wherever he can succeed in introducing discord, he is sure to obtain an easy victory. You are all members of the same household, all so necessary to each other, that alone, not one of you can accomplish any thing, and you ought to cultivate a more kindly feeling even for your own sakes. Rhetoric! do help us to change the subject; you generally have something agreeable to say.

RHETORIC.

I dreamed a dream,
A glorious dream,
Of the wondrous olden times;
I heard a sound,
A thrilling sound,
As of ancient Christmas chimes;
And a world of thought
In my heart then wrought,
Till a tumult of magic chords
Burst like music out,
With a joyous shout,
In a shower of burning words.
Then curious tropes,
Told of golden hopes
And metaphors came in crowds;
So I sat to write
In the joyous light
Tho' I noticed the distant clouds.
To my sisters three
Who preceded me
My gratitude long shall last;

They have helped me well,
As I'm proud to tell,
Though my school days now are past.

FOLLY.

Well, really this is too touching! it is too much for my
delicate nerves. Those exquisite sentiments couched in
those equally exquisite verses penetrate my sensitive sys-
tem too deeply. Excuse my excitement—it is natural to
me. You know my name I am certain : it is Folly—Miss
Fluent Folly of Affectation Street.—Well, those exquisite
lines—they do so remind me of some verses I met with
not long since. I think I recollect them:

Then the beauteous moon,
Like a silver spoon
Gleamed in the milky way;
And its waning light,
From my failing sight
Passed like a dream away.

MADAME LEARNING (aside).

Yes, I knew she would be here and I knew the part
she'd play ; I hate that way of mimicking what is said.
" The moon like a silver spoon indeed ! Who ever heard
of such a comparison ? [Aloud.] History, my dear, you
ought to be able to tell us something interesting : our
kind patrons are anxious to hear you.

HISTORY.

In the old-time nations
When the world was young,
With the muse I wandered
With the muse I sung;
Miriam's song of triumph,
Still methinks I hear;

Homer and Herodotus,
  Both to me so dear.
History my name is,
  Nations are my theme,
Born, progressing, dying,
  Fading like a dream ;
Babylonian glories,
  Persia's purple pride,
And the Hebrew people
  Ruined—deicide !—
Egypt's wonderous monuments,
  Every one I know ;
Carthage, ere the Romans
  Wrought her overthrow ;
Greece, the home of beauty,
  Liberty and song,
Greece ! my chiefest glory,
  I have loved her long ;
Rome, the mighty mistress
  Of the nations all,
Well I know her story
  Her decline and fall :
Poets, warriors, heroes,
  All were hers ; she reigned
Queen of arts and arms,
  Till her shield she stained.
Then God's vengeance sent her
  Tribes unknown before,
Ruin, desolation
  O'er her fields to pour ;
Veiled she sat, and humbled
  Midst her proud old hills,
Till the gospel's triumph
  All her being thrills.

Like the second temple
  Of the ancient law,
Was her later glory;
  Faith enshrined she saw,
Faith triumphant reigning
  Where the gods had reigned;
Victories o'er error
  And o'er evil gained.
Through the modern nations
  Swiftly I career,
Noting all their changes
  With a sort of fear.
France is still the splendid,
  Switzerland the free,
Poland broken-hearted,
  England great on sea!
Russia ever rising,
  Since her great old czar,
Peter, taught the arts of peace
  And the art of war.
Austria declining,
  Since she shared in sin;
Prussia—well, her penance
  Did not yet begin.
O'er the wide Atlantic
  Often do I come,
To record the glories
  Of young Freedom's home:
Names of those who nursed her,
  I am pleased to write;
Washington's—I placed it
  In a blaze of light!
Jefferson and Jackson,
  All her statesmen old,

Have their names recorded
Not in ink but gold;
But her second glory
Will outshine the past,
When the Faith here triumphs,
As it will, at last;
When this mighty people,
One in faith and love,
Labor for God's glory,
Seek their home above.

FOLLY.

Oh! how sweetly that sounds! Really, I never had any intimacy with History until now, and I am perfectly charmed with her.

To be sure I don't care much about these strange, old out-of-the-way places she mentions; but then Europe,—Europe is so fashionable; France!—oh, they make us such sweet dresses in France—so expensive, so beautiful! Oh, I do love France! Then Italy!—I do love the Italian opera: it is so sweet!

Yes, dear History, I admire your taste very much; your last words went to my heart. They reminded me of some lines I once composed myself:—

Yes, the newest fashions
Far outshine the past;
Fashion reigns and revels
There from first to last.
Half the world is governed
By her potent sway,
She can make December
Dress like flowery May.

13

MADAME LEARNING *seems indignant, and says:*
Geography, my dear child, why do you keep our friends
waiting ? You should have followed your sister, History,
without this delay. Madame Folly will pardon me, but
I must do my duty.

GEOGRAPHY.

'Tis not the deeds of passing creatures
   That I discuss ; tis God's creation grand,—
The ocean with its myriad sunny islands,
   By storms shaken, or by soft airs fanned.
The rivers streaming from their far-off fountains
   And bearing health and beauty on their way,
The sun-clad mountain and the green, soft valley,
   The sea-swept headland and the sheltering bay;
The zones I traverse and the grand divisions,
   The continents, the islands and the seas.
Among the tropic fruits I rest at leisure,
   And in the polar regions nearly freeze;
I cross the rude domains of ancient Asia,
   I climb the lofty Himalaya range;
China, Japan, and Tartary, and Thibet
   I view, and start to see some signs of change.
Yet still the Ganges is a sacred river,
   The Indus to the ocean rushes down,
And still the Brahmins rule the castes and cheat them
   In many a quiet Asiatic town.
To Africa I go (dear me, I hate it),
   The desert still is arid as of old,
And Dahomey its hecatombs still offers,
   Congo is savage, and the Coast of Gold.
Egypt, of course, is always well worth noting,
   And I have taken pains about the Nile;
Algeria makes a pretty decent figure,
   Since French industry taught her fields to smile.

Of Europe I am tired—she's too fickle,
    She alters and re-alters all her states;
What's Austria to-day to-morrow's Prussia,—
    They change their boundaries as you change the dates.
But *here*, this land Geography delights in,
    It grows and grows in energy each day;
It finds new rivers, makes new States and names them,
    And fixes them up shipshape right away.
I have a fellow-feeling for my sister,
    Historia—she who spoke before myself,
But Madame Rhetoric in nothing helps me,
    Her tropes and figures I put on the shelf.
As for Dame Folly, I can't help despising
    Her observations and her stupid views:
E'en Ignorance is better—she will listen
    To what you say because she's fond of news.

ASTRONOMY *and* BOTANY *advance together, and seem as if
about to speak, but* IGNORANCE *interposes, and says:*

I can't endure these creatures! What are they talking
about? Places I never heard of, and things not worth a
thought! There's Botany, with her weeds and wild
flowers,—she wants to make a speech about them, no
doubt. Why, Mythology!—I don't see her here fortu-
nately; but I assure you she tells stories more extravagant
than "Sinbad the Sailor," or "Beauty and the Beast."
Astronomy too,—you'll find she is in a way about the
sun, moon, and stars,—things that we can see for ourselves, if we only look up at the right time.

ASTRONOMY.

No, no, indeed! I will be very silent,
    Accustomed to the "music of the spheres;"
I'm stupid here on earth, and very lonely,
    For in the heavens are all my hopes and fears.

My name's Astronomy, I love the starlight,
    The planets and the constellations grand,
I circumnavigate the zodiac often,
    I know the signs, and how the whole was planned.
But I am silent. Botany, my darling,
    Come gather up your petals and your leaves,
I'll send sweet influences down to bless them, —
    Dear little soul, why is it that she grieves?

BOTANY.

    Oh! no, I do not grieve, dear friend;
        I'm happy in the wood,
    Or in the fields, or on the hills, —
        For nature's true and good.
    I only fear Dame Ignorance,
        She seems so very cross,
    I fear she'll crush these petals all
        Or trample on the moss.

PHILOSOPHY.

I have so much to say, so many duties,
    Such various objects tending all to one,
That I would try your patience too severely
    If my account of them were once begun.
I deal in logic, metaphysics, physics,
    And e'en psychology is in my sphere;
So do excuse me, for I have not courage
    To meet the critics that I know are here.

IGNORANCE.

    Phil-e-so-fy is your name, ma'am, I hear. I had a notion
that I heard it before, and I thought I might know you, —
but my friend's name was Phil Brophy, and he dealt in
lumber and lime. What did you say you dealt in? Log-
gerheads was it?—and metal stitches and physic? Well,
I don't think much of your business, ma'am, that's all.

ARITHMETIC.

I've been calculating closely
   The minutes as they fly;
Half an hour is thirty minutes,
   To account for by and by.
Words, when multiplied too often,
   Are a trouble to the soul;
Patience, tortured by division
   Leaves a very scanty whole.
Grace is something very precious;
   If subtracted from by sins,
You will find a small remainder
   When the judgment hour begins.
Virtues done up by addition
   Give a sum I value much,
'Tis a total time can't lessen,
   And that death itself can't touch.
Yet, if tried by long division,
   It may lessen by degrees,
As the water, in mid-winter
   Left exposed, will surely freeze.
Thus Arithmetic would warn you,
   Young or old, or grey or gay,
Using thus her terms, they'll help you
   To ascend the "narrow way."

FOLLY.

Oh! I remember some verses just like these:—

   Tell me what's the price of music
      At fifty cents per note,
   Counting all the semiquavers
      While their sounds around you float.
   Tell me just how many flowers
      It would take to trim a hat,

Whose circumference is equal
To a saucer's lying flat ?

RELIGION.

I come, uncalled-for, yet you'll bid me welcome!
    For Learning always was my kindest friend;
If rightly used and rightly comprehended,
    We help each other to attain one end.
I am Religion, grave perhaps, and thoughtful,
    Yet happy-hearted, and for ever young,
Ever the same when thorns bestrew my pathway
    As when green palms or flowers are o'er it flung.
I would be all to all, gay with the children,
    Yet full of sympathy with those that weep;
For well I know the ills of life are often,
    For mere earth-sympathies, too fine, too deep.
I would be all to all—would keep the youthful
    Free from all sorrow, safe from every sin;
Would suffer no rude hand to pluck the flowers
    That strew the pathway where young lives begin.
I would be all to all—would lead the aged
    Near to the altar, nearer to the Lord,
Would make them rich in graces and in blessings,
    And soothe their sorrows with His gracious word.
I would be all to all—would win God's creatures
    To the sweet love of His most Sacred Heart:
Would bind them there with fetters of His forging
    And make them happy with love's own dear art.
And now, farewell! Remember that no learning
    Can bring you happiness when far from me,
And that Religion is your only safeguard—
    With her you're happy, and with her you're free.

FINIS.

www.ingramcontent.com/pod-product-compliance
Lightning Source LLC
Chambersburg PA
CBHW031401270326
41929CB00010BA/1280